KILVERT'S CORNISH DIARY

For Peter and Elizabeth

KILVERT'S
CORNISH DIARY

JOURNAL NO. 4, 1870

FROM JULY 19TH TO AUGUST 6TH.

CORNWALL

edited by

Richard Maber
and Angela Tregoning

ALISON HODGE

First published in 1989 by Alison Hodge
Bosulval, Newmill, Penzance, Cornwall
TR20 8XA

British Library Cataloguing in Publication Data
Kilvert, Francis, 1840–1879
Kilvert's Cornish diary: 19 July – 6 August 1870
1. Church of England. Kilvert, Francis, 1840–1879
I. Title II. II. Maber, Richard
III. Tregoning, Angela
283′092′4
ISBN 0-906720-19-2

Designed and originated in-house.
Set in ITC Garamond.
Printed and bound by BPCC Wheatons Ltd, Exeter

Contents

Introduction

This is the first complete edition of one of only three surviving original notebooks of Francis Kilvert's Diary. The sad story of the fate of this work contains several mysteries, but so far as it is known it can be briefly told.

Kilvert began his Diary on 1 January 1870, in his thirtieth year, and kept it continuously until at least 13 March 1879. When he began he was curate of Clyro, near Hay-on-Wye in the Welsh borders, and had already been there since 1865. In 1872 he moved to be curate to his father, the Rector of Langley Burrell in Wiltshire. He was subsequently Vicar of St Harmon, near Rhayader, from 1876 to 1877, when he accepted the living of Bredwardine in Herefordshire; and there he died on 23 September 1879, at the age of 38, and only five weeks after his marriage.

It is thought that at the time of Kilvert's death his Diary filled as many as 27–30 notebooks. His widow Elizabeth seems to have removed, for personal reasons, all the notebooks covering two lengthy periods (9 September 1875 – 1 March 1876, and 27 June 1876 – 31 December 1877), and presumably any written after the last known entry. Other more minor acts of censorship were also carried out, probably (but not certainly) by her, such as pages removed and holes cut in the text. When she died in 1911 the 22 remaining notebooks passed to Dora Pitcairn, Kilvert's younger sister, and she in turn left them to her nieces Florence and Essex Smith. In 1937 their brother Perceval submitted them to the publishers Jonathan Cape, whose reader, the poet William Plomer, immediately recognized their quality.

Plomer edited three volumes of selections from the Diary in 1938–41, printing in all about one-third of the surviving text (hereafter referred to as *Kilvert's Diary*). On Perceval's death the notebooks returned to his sister Essex, now Mrs Hope, and at some date before 1955 she apparently destroyed all except three. These three are consecutive, and date from the first year of the Diary: they are numbered by Kilvert as Nos. 2, 3, and 4. The first, covering the period 27 April – 10 June 1870, was given to the playwright Jeremy Sandford; the second (11 June – 18 July) to Mr Charles Harvey of Birmingham; and the third to William Plomer. The first two are now in the National Library of Wales (referred to as *NLW 1* and *NLW 2*); while the third, the present volume, was bequeathed by Plomer to Durham University Library along with his other literary papers.

This notebook is entirely concerned with a holiday spent in Cornwall, and Kilvert has deliberately arranged it so as to make it self-contained: it begins at 11.35 a.m. on 19 July 1870 as he catches the down train, and ends at 11.05 a.m. on 6 August as he catches the train back. Even though Plomer prints a long entry for the rest of that day, a nostalgic and sentimental effusion on the return journey, this must have been written in the next notebook: the final four blank leaves have been carefully removed from the 'Cornish' journal, to increase the sense of its being a separate unity.

Kilvert's hosts in Cornwall were his friends William and Emma Hockin. William Hockin, the son of a former Vicar of Stithians and Perranarworthal, is described on his marriage certificate as 'Gentleman', and on their eldest son's birth certificate as 'Railway Shareholder'. He was 32; Emma Kate (née Baines) was 26. They were married on 1 January 1867 in Dulwich, and rented Langley Lodge, Langley Burrell – Kilvert's father's parish – from March 1867 until their move to Cornwall around March 1869, after William inherited the property of Tullimaar.

It is not known whether either of them knew any of the Kilverts before they came to Langley Burrell:

1 Revd Francis Kilvert.

some of the diarist's references to Emma have prompted speculation that he might have known her before her marriage, but there is no direct evidence of this. The two families had clearly become good friends. William and Emma Hockin were staying in Langley Rectory in June 1870, when Emma and Kilvert's sister Dora laid out a 'new shrubbery walk' (see *NLW 2*, entries for 11 June and 17 July), and Dora seems already to have visited Tullimaar before his own stay there.

By then the Hockins had two children, Ernest Frederick, born in Langley Burrell on 14 December 1867, and Florence Mary, born on 24 April 1869. Their third child, Beatrice Emma, was born on 10 February 1871, which means that Emma was two and a half months pregnant at the time of Kilvert's visit. To his intense delight, Kilvert was asked to be Beatrice's godfather. Two other children followed, Lancelot Cuthbert Baines (whom Kilvert baptized) in 1872, and Kathleen Margaret in 1877. A number of later visits between the friends are recorded in the published extracts of the Diary, the last being when William and Emma stayed in Langley Burrell in April 1876. Emma Hockin died suddenly in 1890, aged 46; William later remarried, and died aged 77 in 1916.

Tullimaar, in Perranarworthal parish, is a handsome house with some eight acres of grounds in a fine situation overlooking Restronguet Creek. It was built in 1828 or 1829 at a cost of over £5,000 by Benjamin Sampson, who grew rich as owner and manager of a powder factory at Cosawes, and was also 'managing partner' of the Perran Foundry at Perranwharf, Perranarworthal. Eventually, following a disputed will, the house passed to William Hockin, who was Sampson's great-nephew. However, the Hockins' stay was a short one. Sampson had acquired the land for Tullimaar from the Basset estate on a lease covering the longest of three lives, a system which did allow for extension by nominating new lives to replace those that died. Unfortunately, though, this does not seem to have been done, and it is thought that when the last life (one Richard Hockin) expired around 1871 the land reverted to the Basset estate, and the Hockins had to leave. The house remains very much as Kilvert knew it, and most of the features that he mentions can still be traced in the grounds.

The first reference to Kilvert's proposed holiday in Cornwall comes in the very first entry of the previous notebook, on Saturday 11 June, when he received a letter from Dora in Langley Burrell and summarized its contents: 'The Hockins propose a driving tour round the Cornish Coast whilst I am with them. This will be delightful' (*NLW 2*, p.1). They carried out their plan with an energy and resourcefulness that are astonishing, even without the added detail of Emma's pregnancy. Saturdays and Sundays were always spent at Tullimaar, but every other day was devoted to excursions short and long, with the sole exception of Thursday 4 August, spent quietly at home after the remarkable two-day trip

2 William Hockin, 'H.', c. 1869–71.

3 Miss Charlotte Hockin, of the Truro Hockins.

to Tintagel; as Kilvert notes, 'A quiet day, and I am sure Mrs H. must have needed one'.

They travelled by a combination of train and horse-drawn vehicles. Some of the days were very long, and they achieved feats of tourism that would be daunting even today. For example on Thursday 21 July they breakfasted at 6.45, then travelled to Hayle and Phillack, walking over the towans and dining there at 2 p.m., before going on to St Mi-

chael's Mount, then back to Hayle and returning by train; while the very next day, after an 8.30 breakfast, they went for some fifty miles over the Lizard peninsula in a horse-drawn carriage, visiting Mullion and Mullion Cove (and walking over to Polurrian), then to Kynance ('late in the afternoon'), and the Lizard, not getting home until 11 p.m. The 'grand expedition to the Land's End' (Wednesday 27 July) is comparable: they caught the 7.35 train

*4 Miss Susan Hockin, H.'s aunt,
housekeeper at Phillack.*

*5 Revd Frederick Hockin, Rector of
Phillack and Gwithian.*

from Perranwell to Penzance, then on in a waggonette and pair, the gentlemen walking all round the coast from St Levan to the Land's End, and finally back late from Penzance by train. When they went to Gurnard's Head on Friday 29 July (travelling via Camborne, itself a two-hour drive from Tullimaar, then a round trip taking in Zennor and Penzance), they did not arrive home until 3 in the morning. The *pièce de résistance* is Tintagel. After spending the night in Lostwithiel (and walking out to Restormel Castle the previous evening), they go from Lostwithiel to Tintagel via Bodmin and Camelford, spend hours clambering over the castle and cliffs, then return to Lostwithiel in their waggonette, and back to Truro the same night by train.

Kilvert clearly regarded his stay in Cornwall as something special, and outside the normal run of experience. The motif of the dream runs right through this notebook, and is repeatedly established in the description of his journey through Devon, with beautiful, evocative pictures of the 'vision of the dim dreamy blue sea': 'Boats with white and red sails skimming across the bay, or lying at anchor like boats in a dream, the shadow glassed in the still unrippled sea so that the shadow looked as tangible and real as the reality'. When he arrives at Tullimaar it is 'the fulfilment of the two years' dream'; the visit to Land's End is 'the accomplishment of an old dream'; and Tintagel is 'the dream come true'. In such a mood he creates some memorable images of natural beauty, and his own response to it, as on the sea-shore at Kynance (a passage omitted by Plomer):

> The retreating tide lapped against the feet of the marble cliffs, stirring and lifting the long seaweed about the rocks. The sun was sinking behind the vast rock called the Asparagus Island. Round the dark rock edges brightened the aureole, and the light came softened and mellowed into the Cove. Between the guardian giant rocks, spaces of deep blue rippling sea, and white sails disappearing behind one rock and emerging again to pass behind another. The splendour of the place, the gorgeous blue and beauty of the broad sea, the coloured rocks, the towering cliffs, the coast, the golden swimming mellow light amongst the huge dark rock masses, indescribable.

This sense of the uniqueness of his Cornish experience reaches its climax in the emotional passage on the return journey which begins the next notebook of the Diary: 'Ah! that was happiness, how great, unbroken sunshine, unclouded blue, too intoxicating, not recognized or valued enough till it was gone' (*Kilvert's Diary*, I, p.208).

So many tourists, in the nineteenth century just as now, came to Cornwall looking for unspoilt beauty, picturesque scenery and an old-world way of life; and Kilvert is no exception. A good part of this notebook is naturally concerned with his visits to what had already become the standard tourist sites. He is very unusual, though, in the way in which he describes what he sees. Far from being conventional or predictable, Kilvert's account of Cornwall is highly individual. It is most instructive to compare his descriptions with those of other Victorian travel writers, or contemporary guide-books. Everything that Kilvert writes is presented through his own eyes and marked with his own personality – with his enthusiasms and his prejudices, his alert observation, and his art of capturing precisely those unexpected details that transform an otherwise familiar scene.

These evocative details are as liable to be unromantic and industrial as more obviously picturesque, and such odd juxtapositions are a striking feature of his picture of Cornwall. The legendary and romantic Cornwall of Tennyson and Bottrell co-exists with the realities of the tourist trade and the facts of rural life; and particularly, with the intense mining and engineering activity that had caused Cornwall to play so prominent a part in the Industrial Revolution. One should not forget that many areas were more industrial in 1870 than now; indeed, within sight of Tullimaar on Restronguet Creek was the chimney of the huge Perran iron foundry. Kilvert vividly depicts these contrasts from the moment his train first crosses the Tamar, and thereafter there are many memorable brief sketches of scenes that other tourists and guide books ignore or pass over hastily – such as the mining area round Redruth: 'The bowels of the earth ripped open, turned inside out in the search for metal ore, the land defiled and cumbered with heaps and wastes of slag and rubbish, and the waters poisoned with tin and copper washings ...'; or the picture of Hayle: 'Walked through the ugly town half seaport, half manufacture, and crossed a dreary creek by a bridge over which runs a tramway for coal &c. The tide was low and the wastes of sand and mud festered and sweltered in the hot sun ...'. Again, as Kilvert's party return from the Lizard late at night, 'the red flames burst and roared from the tops of the tall mine chimneys'. Similar details are noted everywhere they go: the new Scilly cable building at Nanjizal Cove, the colliers at Portreath, the great St Ives Consols mine on the way to Zennor, the stamps on the Red River between Gwithian and Godrevy, and the iron mine near Restormel Castle. Even at Tintagel, the holy of holies for the romantic tourist, Kilvert notes that 'they have just begun mining for iron in this cliff'.

Cornwall in 1870 was not at all a static society, but was in the middle of a dramatic phase of development. Although the traditional industries of mining and engineering seem to Kilvert to be thriving, this prosperity was in fact largely illusory. There had been a severe depression in the 1860s (reflected in the Diary by the abandoned tin-stamping works in Nanjizal Bay that Kilvert described on the way to Land's End). Then a sharp rise in the price of tin caused a short-lived boom in the early 1870s, but this was soon followed by a catastrophic recession from which Cornwall never recovered. A straw in the wind was the collapse of the famous Cornish Copper Company at Hayle: Riviere House and estate at Phillack, which the diarist visits on 21 July, had just been purchased from the defunct company at a bargain price by his host's uncle, the Revd Frederick Hockin. This decade brought the phenomenon of a wave of emigration of astonishing proportions, which was compared at the time to that from Ireland during the Great Famine, and which profoundly changed the nature of Cornwall. The census figures tell the story. Against rapidly rising national figures, the population of Cornwall declined from 369,390 in 1861 to an 1871 total of 362,343, and then dropped dramatically to 330,686 in 1881; the lowest point was not reached until 1931 – 317,968 – and even by 1961 it had only recovered to 342,301, some 5.5 per cent less than in Kilvert's day. At the same time as the industrial decline, though, there began the great expansion of the tourist industry, on which the Cornish economy came increasingly to rely, and which is also clearly foreshadowed in Kilvert's notebook.

Thus Kilvert gives us a fascinating picture of a Cornwall balanced between the old and the new: still in many ways the old Cornwall, but already changing rapidly, and presaging a more fundamental transformation. Some of the sights that Kilvert describes were very soon to vanish, such as St Mary's Church in Truro and the old Lanhydrock House; even the great Perran iron foundry was to close in 1879. Yet so much is in reality of very recent date. The restoration of the churches of St Michael Penkevil, Mullion, Tintagel, and Gwithian; the docks at Falmouth and the impressive new hotel, built specifically to accomodate tourists brought by the railway, with all that that portended for the future; the lifeboat house at Mullion, the Scilly telegraph and the Wolf Rock lighthouse: none dated back more than about five years, and many were brand new. Indeed, the railway itself had only come to Perranwell as recently as 1863.

If Kilvert avoids some of the usual selective vision of the tourist, it is because of his alert curiosity and fascination with every aspect of the world around him. The same qualities inspire his attitude to the people that he meets, and whom he describes in the pages of his Cornish diary.

In Clyro Kilvert's position as curate enabled him to move with ease in every sphere of society, from the landed gentry to the poor in the villages and farms. He brings the same breadth of human interest to recording his experiences in Cornwall. His position as guest inevitably means that he spends most of his time with the Hockin family in Tullimaar, Phillack, or Truro, or with the Parkers of Rosewarne and their friends. But he seems to treat all those whom he meets as individuals, whatever their social status, often noting their names or recording their very words: as with the Truro boatman, Eliza Killing the nurse, Martin the groom, Richard Tresidder the gardener, Edward Noy the Penzance driver, and Mary Mundy the innkeeper of Mullion. He also paints miniature portraits of such very different guides as those he met with at the Mount ('the pretty delicate gentle melancholy girl'), the Logan Rock ('his action was so sudden, strange and wild, and so exactly that of a monkey clambering up the bars of his cage, that I looked to see whether he had a tail'), and Tintagel ('an old man with a red face ... hobbling round the garden with a stick').

Although the period covered by the Cornish notebook is only nineteen days, there is a great deal of drama in these pages. Kilvert's stay in Cornwall encompassed a shipwreck on the Stags' Horns (20 July and 22 July), an illegal wedding at Phillack, a young man drowning at Hayle (both 21 July), and the discovery of the bodies of babies in the roof of the Market Jew Street Chapel in Penzance (27 July).

In addition, he reports a considerable number of other dramatic stories that he has been told, of violent death (the fight between the conger and the seal; the walled-in skeleton in the Mount; Captain Opie's fatal fall from the omnibus; the drowning of the curate Drury at Gwithian), or exciting escapes (the young man at the Funnel Rock; the unexplained references to the St Ives lifeboat men and the escape from drowning in New Zealand). In this way the scope of reference is extended far beyond the simple account of a pleasant holiday, and a much wider time-scale is conveyed than the short period of Kilvert's stay. Equally, it is amusing to see how Kilvert includes lively descriptions of things that he has *not* actually experienced. An extreme case is his note on the way to Land's End: 'nearer shore rode the bell buoy, but we could not hear the solemn incessant tolling of the bell'; and both at Phillack and at the Land's End he recounts amazing anecdotes of violent tempests on the wild coast, so different from the flat calm that, to his disappointment, he actually saw. In all these ways, he is deliberately heightening the interest of his diary.

Even so, Kilvert does not write down everything that he does see, or everything that he is told. There are some surprising omissions in this journal – he describes Carn Brea Castle but not the Monument, and at Land's End the Wolf Rock lighthouse but not the Longships – and others are commented on in the notes. It might seem rather speculative to suppose that he must have been told anecdotes that he does not record, but there is good evidence for this later in the Diary. To give a Cornish example, on Sunday 27 August 1871 Kilvert tells the splendid anecdote of how an earlier tenant of Tullimaar went picturesquely mad during Communion in the church of St Michael Penkevil at Tregothnan: 'At dinner tonight I told Roland Venables the story that Hockin told me about poor Lanyon who used to live at Tullimaar ...'(*Kilvert's Diary*, II, pp.22–3). Now he must himself have been told this story when the Hockins visited Langley Burrell on 15–16 August that year, if not even at the time of his own visit to Cornwall in 1870. It is curious, but entirely consistent with the relative flexibility of his diary-keeping habits, that he should not have recorded the anecdote when he first heard it, but did include it later when he retailed it himself. Similarly in the Cornish notebook, there is good reason to suppose that Kilvert must have been told the strange story of the curate of Gwithian's dream of his own death (see Notes to Friday 5 August), and it is inconceivable that he should not have known the extraordinary background to the Parkers' residence at Rosewarne (see Notes to Wednesday 27 July); yet there is no hint of either in the text. The Diary is not such a straightforward document as it might appear.

All diaries are two-way mirrors, reflecting the world through the diarist's eyes, and the diarist himself through his own words. Our picture of the writer is itself built up in quite a complex way. In part, a diary represents a conscious effort at self-revelation – or the creation of an image that the diarist wishes to present of himself – and in part, the self-revelation is unconscious, and not always perhaps what the writer might have wished.

We learn a good deal about Kilvert from this Cornish notebook, which is all the more valuable in that he is away from his familiar background of Clyro or Langley Burrell. For example his love of Wales, and identification with its people, shines through these pages. Even as he travels down through Devon he notes that 'these beautiful *combes* reminded me of our own *cwms* and dingles in Wales'. The possessive adjective here is revealing, and entirely typical, and thereafter it is to Wales, rather than to his native England, that he compares most of the distinctive features of Cornwall: the Cornish hills are like those of Radnorshire, the Cornish people are 'much taller larger people than the Welsh', the heather on the Lizard peninsula is 'growing as freely as gorse grows with us', and so on throughout the notebook. He comments on 25 July 'I find many words, ideas and superstitions and customs kindred to those of Wales', and even spells a Cornish village as though it were Welsh ('Llandewednack'). He is never far in his thoughts from Clyro and its children. At the end of the long entry on Thursday 21 July, describing a day exceptionally full of interest and activity, his final sentence is: 'Today was the Confirmation at Hay, and I thought of the Clyro young people'; and on Friday 29 July at Gurnard's Head, when he sees 'a row of children who were sitting on a wall like a line of seagulls', his first thought is that 'they seemed nice children and reminded me of some of my Clyro pets'.

Equally evident is his affection for animals, and his ability to immortalize them in sharp little vignettes – an attractive aspect of Kilvert's personality, which is reflected elsewhere in the Diary in the revulsion that he feels at blood sports. There are lively descriptions of all the animals at Tullimaar, including Mrs Hockin's two pet toads, who 'make a funny little plaintive squeaking noise when she calls them'; while from Carclew across the creek come the sounds of owls hooting, harriers baying, and deer calling their fawns. There are many examples of such sympathetic observation, as at Riviere House ('a large fierce tall black dog was walking solemnly up and down curling his tail over his back'), or Treen, the 'paradise of black pigs'. Particularly striking is Kilvert's eye for horses, which is evident in many other parts of the Diary. He has a happy knack of finding a phrase to describe the personality of the horses that convey them around Cornwall, from the 'pair of gallant greys' that take them for fifty miles over the Lizard, to their long drive from Lostwithiel to Tintagel and back with 'a game bay horse and a slug of a chestnut mare'.

Kilvert is never diffident in expressing his likes and dislikes, and he reserves an especially effective line of abuse for tourists, as at the Logan Rock ('a rude vulgar crew of tourists ... grinning like dogs') and Land's End ('a noisy rabble of tourists, males and females'), both on 27 July. That he was a tourist himself seems not to have troubled him. He presumably regarded himself and his friends as falling in the same category as the 'gentleman' seeing the sights at St Michael's Mount on 21 July, to whom no objection is made – a category defined in part perhaps by class, and in part by the avoidance of obstreperous behaviour (see below in the Notes to Restormel, 2 August). All the same, he carries out all the rituals expected of the tourist, such as sitting in St Michael's Chair and rocking the Logan Stone, and collects souvenirs of all sorts wherever he goes. It is amusing to contrast Kilvert's strictures on the 'noisy rabble' with his enjoyment of the boisterousness of Captain Parker in his own 'very merry party'; and at Gwithian on 5 August his complaints about the dissenting farmer who is ruining the ancient British church come immediately after he has himself taken a piece of pink felspar from the 'almost perfect' walls. Such all-too-human inconsistencies contribute a great deal to the charm of the Diary.

One suspects at times an element of self-parody in Kilvert's exaggerated indignation at tourists and dissenters. Certainly, his sense of humour and fun, with a lively vein of self-mockery, is abundantly clear in the early years of his Diary, and is very well represented in the Cornish notebook. One strand of his humour is consistently omitted by Plomer in his editing of the Diary – that is, Kilvert's liking for schoolboyish puns (for example, 'I wonder how Caesar liked travelling on the top of the diligence (summa diligentia) when he crossed the Alps', 29 July). This is not the only case where the editor has apparently tried to improve the literary tone of the text, and in doing so run a severe risk of distorting its flavour.

Kilvert's language is enriched by frequent literary allusions, either as direct quotations or as semi-submerged references or reminiscences. There is a good deal of biblical language, almost always used humorously, which is hardly surprising in a young curate; and while the frequency with which his mind turns to English poetry is certainly striking, his taste among the poets is entirely predictable: the inevitable Tennyson, and Shakespeare, Milton, Macaulay, Wordsworth, Coleridge, Gray, and Cowper. Such allusions tend to serve as a kind of literary shorthand, evoking a mood through reference to the original context of the quotation: a good example is Kilvert's use of Tennyson at Tintagel, to give an air of romantic mystery to his visit.

On occasion they can give us a glimpse of a darker side of Kilvert's character than that which he felt able to reveal openly in his Diary. There are a number of odd and unexplained remarks in this journal, usually in a surprising context, and so enigmatic as to be almost impossible to explain ('Sorrowful dreams' in Redruth market; '"The last sigh of the moon"' at Godrevy). In one outstanding case, though, a literary reference provides the key to one of the most unexpected and explicit pieces of self-revelation to have survived in the entire Diary. On 24 July, on a quiet Sunday afternoon at Tullimaar, Kilvert and the Hockins had coffee in the summer house and sat talking before Evensong; and the diarist adds: "'Aside the devil turned &c. &c. –" Ah, how intelligible'. The reference seems to have eluded all subsequent readers: it comes from Book IV of *Paradise Lost*, as Satan gazes in furious jealousy at the physical happiness of Adam and Eve, and is consumed with frustrated lust and unfulfilled desire. There is not a trace of irony or self-mockery in this brief and unexpanded personal note, which perhaps gives a hint as to what some of the lost parts of the Diary might have contained. It certainly supports the view that some of the unexplained tensions and restless energy evident in the Diary – and perhaps also the later hints of depression – might have had their origins in Kilvert's state of reluctant celibacy. The whole passage is given in the Notes; Plomer omitted the entire day's entry in his edition.

As such a passage suggests, a major source of interest and linking thread through this notebook is Kilvert's developing relationship with Emma Hockin, whose lively and charming personality is vividly conveyed. We can follow as, consciously or not, his affection for her deepens into something approaching infatuation, while she too was clearly not indifferent to the handsome and enthusiastic young clergyman. He was probably unaware of how revealing his own writing is of his feelings: he constantly reports on what she says and does; in her absence (as on the walk round the coast to Land's End) he longs for her to be there to share the experience; and even his account of a musical evening (4 August) seems to be unconsciously coloured by his emotional state. It is interesting to contrast Kilvert's tone when writing of Emma just before his trip to Cornwall with the hyperbolic despair of his thoughts on the return journey. In the previous notebook he writes with affectionate pleasure: 'Got home just in time to write to Mrs Hockin to ask when she expects me at Tullimaar. She alludes to me in her letter to my Mother as "Frank" and I think it is very friendly and nice of her' (*NLW 2*, 7 July); while just a month later his tone is very different: 'All through the journey my eyes were perpetually seeking for the one familiar face and form which have been so constantly before them for the last three weeks, seeking, seeking, baffled, longing, all in vain ... And the wretchedness, the utter misery, of the blank and the continual disappointment ... I thought – was it so – that there were tears in those blue eyes when we parted. I know there were tears in mine. Forget me not, oh, forget me not' (6 August, *Kilvert's Diary*, I, pp.207–8). One should not, of course, make too much of this, and there can never have been the slightest impropriety: Kilvert was constantly becoming helplessly attracted to pretty young women, and such feelings rarely survived for long. However, there seems little doubt that Emma's presence did much to stimulate the state of heightened sensibility so evident in his perception of Cornwall.

Kilvert's Cornish Diary is in part a travel journal, and in part a far more personal account; from this combination of elements springs much of its distinctiveness. It has in the past been relatively neglected. This is understandable in that most commentators have brought to Kilvert's work a particular love of the Welsh border region of Clyro and Bredwardine, or, to a rather lesser extent, the Langley Burrell area near Chippenham; even William Plomer, to judge from his editing, was very unclear as to the background to this notebook. In reality, though, it is a fascinating document, full of interest – and its share of the unexpected – in the picture that it gives both of Kilvert and of Cornwall.

The Manuscript

Kilvert's Cornish Diary is written in an unremarkable plain notebook measuring 177 x 110 mm, with an embossed black cover. The pages are lined, and correctly numbered 1–180 in ink; four leaves have been neatly cut out from the end of the notebook, so that there are no blank pages after the end of the text. In format it is identical to the other two surviving notebooks, the only exterior difference being that the first of these (*NLW 1*, MS 21666A) is very dark red rather than black.

On the inside front cover William Plomer has written the following:'MS Notebook of the Diary of the Revd. Francis Kilvert for 1870 (19 July – 6 August) describing his visit to the Hockins in Cornwall. This was presented to W.P. at Worthing on 16 Sept. 1958 by Mrs Essex Hope (née Smith), Kilvert's niece. She said she had destroyed all but three of the original 22 MS Notebooks. This one was given to me. Another was given some time ago to one Jeremy Sandford, living in Herefordshire. I don't know what happened to the third. W.P. 17.9.58.' On a blank page opposite the first page of text, there is the heading in Kilvert's hand:'Journal. No. 4. 1870. From July 19th. to August 6th. Cornwall.'

The text does not follow continuously throughout the notebook. Each day begins on a new page, and sometimes a full page has been left blank between two entries, while a considerable number of gaps also intersperse the individual entries. Of the 180 pages in the notebook, 12 are completely blank, and a further 36 contain blank spaces extending to at least a quarter of the page, many of them very substantial. In addition, there are around 90 instances of gaps in the text extending to 1–4 ruled lines. Sometimes Kilvert is marking different phases of a day's entry, but very often he has clearly left spaces to be filled in later with further details of his activities; occasionally, he has run out of space when filling in such a gap. Such blank pages, and spaces left within a day's entry, are also found in the other two surviving notebooks (for example the entry for 18 May in *NLW 1*, or the very disjointed one for 13 July in *NLW 2*), but they are much more frequent in the Cornish Diary.

This notebook, like the other two, tells us a great deal about how Kilvert wrote his diary, and we can follow the successive stages through which the text has evolved. There is good evidence elsewhere that

6 and 7 Pages from the Diary.

he took a pocket-book with him when he went out, to jot down notes, incidents, and little vignettes, which no doubt accounts for the detached but vivid isolated observations frequently found in the entries. The next stage was a first rough draft of at least the more extended passages of a day's entry, which would then have been copied up into the notebook (this is shown by the fact that the diarist's eye sometimes slipped while copying, and a missing word or phrase had to be supplied later to make sense) – he twice describes himself as 'writing' in his room early in the morning before breakfast (25 July and 2 August).

There are a good number of erasures in the text, where the surface of the paper has been scraped away, and the correction usually written over the top. In several cases the original word can still be made out; in almost all of these it was a copying slip

8 and 9 Pages from the Diary.

that Kilvert has corrected on the spot. A day's entry was not always copied up at one sitting, and there are changes of ink and angle of writing. Once, indeed, Kilvert closed the notebook too hastily while the ink was still wet (perhaps because interrupted?); but the ink marks on the opposite page only extend half-way down the page, showing how far he had got at that point (pages 154–5 of the notebook, in the description of Tintagel Castle). He has several times left small spaces to fill in later, usually where he is unsure of a proper name. When the missing detail was added, it rarely filled the space exactly, while sometimes these spaces have been filled by a different hand, and several were never completed (examples are mentioned in the Notes). Finally, on reading over the text Kilvert has quite frequently added to it, often with qualifying adjectives, or phrases and even whole sentences inserted and squeezed in between lines. More extended after-thoughts have occasionally been appended at the end of a day's entry, or in one of the spaces left in the text, so that a strict chronological sequence is not always observed. Most of these features can be seen on the photographs of the manuscript.

The vertical lines visible in the margins of the manuscript are red crayon marks made by William Plomer to indicate the passages to be omitted from his edition (when whole days were omitted he underlined in red the date at the beginning). Plomer published only about one-third of the Cornish diary, roughly the same proportion as with the other two surviving notebooks (in *NLW 2*, 15 out of the 34 days covered were omitted in their entirety), and apparently the same throughout the whole Diary. He did, however, make available to the Kilvert Society a transcript of the other passages, and these were issued in 1978 in a duplicated typescript pamphlet (*Kilvert's Cornish Holiday: further extracts from Kilvert's Diary, July 19th to August 6th 1870*, Hay-on-Wye, 1978). Even so, there are a number of omissions from the manuscript text. Plomer's reading of the manuscript is not reliable: there are over one hundred misreadings or omissions in the text of this notebook alone. Most of them are fairly minor; but nevertheless, the cumulative effect is to present a text which differs persistently from what Kilvert wrote.

Kilvert's handwriting, although neat, is not always easy to read, and has several idiosyncrasies, the most striking being his habit of dotting the letter 'e' as well as 'i'. His punctuation is minimal, and not at all systematic. In establishing this edition we have kept as close as possible to the original text, but have added punctuation (mainly commas) where necessary to facilitate reading, and in a very few cases have regularized the spelling. Spaces in the text are represented by an extra space between paragraphs; while other significant features are commented on in the Notes.

Acknowledgements

The research for this edition has been carried out in a number of institutions, and we would like to record our thanks for the unfailing assistance and co-operation that we have received from librarians and curators. Special thanks are due to Miss E.M. Rainey, Keeper of Rare Books of Durham University Library, and David Burnett, Assistant Librarian, for their constant help; the Librarian of the National Library of Wales, and particularly Dafydd Ifans, who allowed us to consult the other two surviving Kilvert notebooks, including the unpublished Harvey notebook, and much other unpublished material; Roger Penhallurick of the Royal Institution of Cornwall, Truro; Terry Knight of the Cornish Studies Library, Redruth; Professor Charles Thomas and Oliver Padel of the Institute of Cornish Studies, Pool; and all the staff at these institutions. Also the following: the British Library, including the Map Room and the Music Library; the Public Record Office; the Cornwall County Record Office, Truro; Hereford Public Library; and Penlee House Museum and Art Gallery, Penzance.

We owe an especial debt to Barry Smith of Truro, who read the typescript and made many invaluable suggestions; to John Hockin of Swanage, grandson of Kilvert's hosts William and Emma, who generously put at our disposal his own extensive researches into his family history; and to Michael Trinick who read the typescript and generously allowed us to reproduce paintings and photographs. We have benefited from the knowledge of many members of the Kilvert Society, and above all of the Society's Secretary, Edward West, and Archivist, Godfrey Davies. We also wish particularly to thank the following for local information: Leslie and Janet Dale, of Churchtown Farm, Perranarworthal; D.M. Laity of Flushing; David Thomas of Camborne; Vivian and Jane Tregoning of Cubert; and Russell and Diana Webber of St Erth. Finally, we are grateful to Mrs Sheila Hooper, the owner of the manuscript copyright, for her encouragement and support for this edition; to Bob Berry for his excellent and painstaking photographic work, and to Carole Page who drew the map.

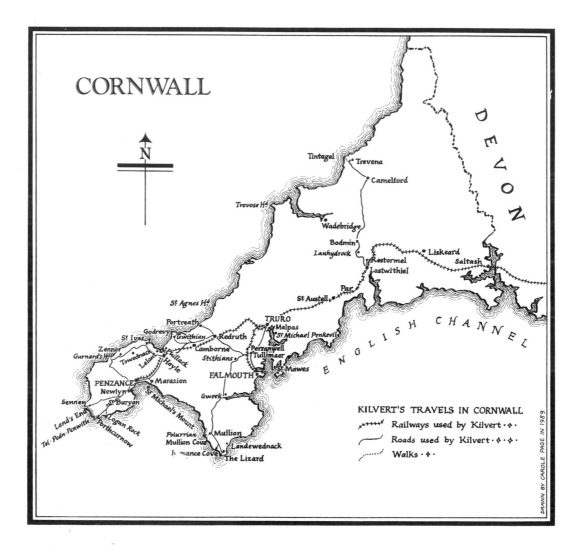

CORNWALL

N

DEVON

Tintagel
Trevena
Camelford
Trevose Hd
Wadebridge
Bodmin
Lanhydrock
Liskeard
Restormel
Lostwithiel
Saltash
Par
St Austell
St Agnes Hd
ENGLISH CHANNEL
Portreath
TRURO
Godrevy
Malpas
St Ives
Gwithian
Redruth
St Michael Penkevil
Zennor
Camborne
Perranwell
Gurnard's Hd
Towednack
Stithians
Tullimaar
Lelant
Phillack
St Mawes
Hayle
Marazion
FALMOUTH
PENZANCE
Newlyn
Gweek
Sennen
St Buryan
St Michael's Mount
Land's End
Logan Rock
Mullion
Tol·Pedn·Penwith
Porthcurnow
Polurrian
Mullion Cove
Landewednack
Kynance Cove
The Lizard

KILVERT'S TRAVELS IN CORNWALL
╈╈╈╈╈╈ Railways used by Kilvert · ✧ ·
─────── Roads used by Kilvert · ✧ · ✧ ·
··········· Walks · ✧ ·

DRAWN BY CAROLE PAGE IN 1989

KILVERT'S
CORNISH DIARY

JOURNAL NO. 4, 1870.

FROM JULY 19TH TO AUGUST 6TH.

CORNWALL.

Tuesday, 19 July, 1870

Left Chippenham 11.35 by the down mail with a tourist ticket for Truro. The carriage full and hot to Bristol, which relieved us of some passengers. From Weston Junction we caught a glimpse of Weston and the dim sea. Then the tall white Burnham lighthouse among the green trees. Windmills whirling. I looked out for the white sails of boats passing up and down the Parret to and from Bridgewater and Burnham, but there were none to be seen. Perhaps the tide was out. Sometimes these white sails may be seen gliding along above the flat green meadows, and, the river being invisible, they look as if the boats were sailing on land.

The next things worth looking at were the long blue waving ranges of the Mendips and Quantocks, left and right of the line, and at Taunton the superb tower of St Mary's with its glorious cluster of pinnacles rising above the masses of green elms against the blue hills beyond, surely the grandest tower in the three Western Shires. The train

10 Exeter Cathedral stands picturesquely above the river.

stopped opposite the Church just in the right place and gave us a view of the magnificent tower between two elm clumps. The country seemed terribly dry burnt and brown above Taunton. Below that they seemed to have had more rain, and the fields looked greener. The train was 20 minutes behind time in reaching Exeter. I had quite forgotten the look of the light airy elegant station. I had the dimmest recollection of Exeter Cathedral and I was much disappointed in it. At first sight it reminds one of a long barn with a squat tower on each side. The Cathedral and the town however stand picturesquely above the river and the great mud flats at the mouth of the Exe. Exmouth lay bright in sunshine across the wide shallow estuary, stranded boats, white sails hovering about the river mouth, a vision of the dim dreamy blue sea beyond and children on the mud flats in the foreground between the railroad and river, boys and girls with their trousers and frocks tucked up paddling in the mud or stalking along with their naked legs through the mud-pools and shallow water as if looking for something. As we neared Starcross, the dim blue of the sea deepened into a soft dreamy blue. The sea was as smooth and shining as glass, scarcely rippled even by the flowing tide, except close to the shore where the little blue waves feathered and crested with white foam for a moment balanced and then plunged over with a slight roar. At Dawlish the sound of the sea was like the rustle of myriads of aspens, a walking, a going in the tops of the aspens.

I remembered Dawlish well, the beach, the piers, the little town divided by the little river, the red cliffs crowned with green meadows (especially the arched rock) and the houses facing the sea, and I fancied I could pick out the house where we lodged many years ago, and I wondered whether the children in the house were speculating as we used to do on the name of the coming engine. People sitting on the sands, some men bathing, the brilliant contrast of the bright red cliffs, green meadows, yellow corn fields, blue sea and sky. Boats with white and red sails skimming across the bay, or lying at anchor like boats in a dream, the shadow glassed in the still unrippled sea so that the shadow looked as tangible and real as the reality. We went flying without stopping through short tunnels bored in the red sandstone rock.

Below Teignmouth all was new to me. These beautiful *combes* reminded me of our own *cwms* and dingles in Wales. Near Totnes in a small meadow very green three men stood staring at the train, with fishing rods quivering in the air. They had plainly just been fishing, probably for trout, in the pretty little brook that skirted the meadow. At Plymouth we were very late, nearly half an hour, and the ordinary train, unable to wait any longer, had been sent on and we were soon dispatched after it in a special train. I had after all missed seeing the Ivy Bridge viaduct. But there were some viaducts further on, quite as lofty and remarkable and made of timber, immense beams supported by other beams upright, bolted together by threes at the bottom but spreading as they rise and reach the floor of the viaduct. After crossing the great Saltash Bridge and the main stream of the Tamar, there seemed to be

11 The great Saltash Bridge.

any number of muddy creeks or tributary branches of the great river, crossed by long lofty
timber bridges. The Cornish mail carriages bear
the Prince of Wales' plume and motto. The first
few miles of Cornwall looked bleak, barren and
uninteresting, the most striking feature being
the innumerable mine works of lead, tin, copper &c crowning the hills with their tall
chimneys, shafts and ugly white dreary buildings, or nestling in a deep narrow valley defiling
and poisoning the streams with the white tin
washings. The country soon grew prettier, the
prevailing feature of the landscape being low

12 Moorswater Viaduct.

rounded hills like those of Radnorshire, divided by very deep narrow valleys or ravines
which the great timber viaducts crossed continually at a ghastly height in the air. The
hill sides were clothed with a rich luxuriance of wood, chiefly oak. A man was mow-
ing oats. Purple heather bloomed in great bunches and bushes along the railway
embankments like broom with us. A sea fog, which enveloped the hills like a mist of
small rain and blotted out the distance, crept up the valleys along the streams and rose
against the dark green oakwoods.

H. met me at Truro (where we changed for Perranwell) and drove me in the pony carriage from Perranwell to Tullimaar.

The fulfilment of the two years' dream.

Wednesday, 20 July

Up by 6.30 writing. A thick sea fog driving up Restronguet Creek, the tidal branch of the Fal that flows down the valley just below the house of Tullimaar.

Opposite, luxuriant woods slope down to the river. It is now the "dead of the neaps", and the bed of the creek river which is covered with a flowing full tide at spring tides is now a waste of brown sand and mud with a narrow muddy stream winding down through it. From one bedroom window I look out upon the front of the house and the rich mingling of the purple beech tints with the bright green of the other trees about the lawns and shrubberies. From the other window nothing is to be seen but the trees and side lawn and terraced grey gravelled walks of Tullimaar, the brown sands, mud and shrunk stream of Restronguet, the rich sloping oak woods dark and impervious, rising from the river bed opposite. Down the river beyond the woods may be seen the back of a rounded hill, and up the river the glint of white buildings on the river side, through the trees, the white walls and chimneys of an iron foundry.

13 Perran Foundry.

After breakfast we all went out and strolled about the lawn and gardens. The children, Ernest and Florence, were in the kitchen garden with the nurse Eliza Killing, eating gooseberries. It is a large garden with a good wall against which are peaches, nectarines &c loaded with fruit, not yet ripe. We ate a quantity of gooseberries &c, and Flo the spaniel devoured the skins.

14 Tullimaar.

Tullimaar is bosomed in rare and beautiful trees and shrubs, cork, sumach.

It does not appear at first sight, but this house and some of the neighbouring houses stand on an island. The island home. At ten we went to Truro in the pony carriage, Mrs H. driving. A pretty road, with long hills and fine views back over the country and mining districts from the crests of the hills. Market day at Truro, and the road lively with market folk. The Cornish people seem fine tall folk, especially the women, much taller larger people than the Welsh, and most of them appear to be dark-haired.

The hedges along these fine broad roads are brilliant with purple heather growing in bushes taller and finer than ours in Wales. It seems to be very early here. We shall not have heather in bloom in Wales for another month. Descending the hill into Truro, a glimpse of the white tall monument of Lander the African traveller, a column surmounted by an erect statue. Entering the town the road passes close beneath the monument. Past the ugly cupola Church with round-headed windows, and we drove to the Royal Hotel. I went with Mrs H. into the market where she

15 The Lander monument.

bought some fish, red mullet and whiting, poultry &c. There was a good supply of fish and a number of conger eels, turbot, John Dory, ray &c.

It is a nice market house and all sorts of things are sold there besides eatable provisions, e.g. boots, clothes, earthenware &c.

Then we went to a pastry cook's and bought some Cornish "pasties" for lunch, a sort of turnover, with meat and potatoes inside instead of fruit or preserve. Truro is a nice clean town with water always running down the little channels at the edge of the pavement on either side of the street. The fine old Church of St Mary with its long line of nave and choir of uniform height, and the rich carving and work above the line of perpendicular windows, looked very tempting, but

16 St Mary's Church.

we had not time to go in and see the interior, as the tide was falling fast and we had to embark on the Truro River before the water was too low for a boat to leave the quay. As we waited on the quay for our boat to come round, an old invalid man who had been in the Infirmary for some time and had only just been sent out, was being tenderly helped into a boat off the quay steps and covered up with cloaks in the stern by two or three men. Mrs H. says the Cornish are very kind and neighbourly to each other, especially when they are in

17 Inside St Mary's.

trouble. Certainly these boatmen were very kind to this old infirm man.

We waited some time for our boat. It was broiling hot on the blazing quay and Mrs H. sat down on the steps. The tide was ebbing low before we embarked and dropped down the river with oars and mizen sail between the steaming mudbanks and sand flats leaving Truro town in a dim haze of heat.

Danish and Norwegian ships, three masted vessels, from 200 to 400 tons, were lying anchored lower down the river above and below Malpas. They had brought timber and were waiting to take back miscellaneous cargoes, among other things, tin and copper.

H. and I landed at Malpas, leaving Mrs H. sitting in the boat. We went up a flight of wooden steps and by a winding garden path to a little inn standing by the side of the high road which here runs parallel with the river. We brought down a basket full of ginger beer and pushed off again immediately as the boatman was a temperance man, had not touched beer &c for years, and would not have anything to drink. This boatman was a shrewd fellow, very original with a quaint caustic turn of humour, but very independent and not always over-complimentary in his replies. Mrs H. said to him that she supposed he had put by some money since he had taken the pledge. How was he to put by money, he said. Oh yes, it was likely that he could put by a lot of money with ten children and sometimes not a penny to be earned for five weeks together.

18 Tregothnan from the Fal.

He also remarked quaintly that he had a good many teeth yet to "let out" for beef when he came across it. He was very wrath with Lord Falmouth for his tyranny and meanness in shutting up his park and not allowing any picnics &c in his woods. However the boatman said he would land parties of pleasure on the estate whenever he chose, in defiance of his Lordship.

About Malpas the Fal becomes very pretty, luxuriant oak woods clothing the sides of the hills which slope down to the river. It is a noble river winding and broadening through the wooded hills down to Falmouth and the blue sea. It has been compared to the Rhine, and indeed there is a resemblance. Gentlemen's seats peep out from the woods that embosom them,

19 '... famous places for picnics'.

or crown the wooded cliff like Lord Falmouth's mansion of Tregothnan. There are beautiful coves in shady dells and glades among the trees on the banks of the river all down the stream, famous places for picnics. Creeks, arms and branches of the Fal joined the river here and there on both sides, bringing in the discoloured water of the tin washings. We passed the mouth of the gorge and creek of Restronguet above which stands Tullimaar. There is a ferry called "King Harry's Passage" because, said the boatman, King Harry flying for his life swam his horse across the river here. But he did not know what King Harry it was, nor could we learn.

20 King Harry Ferry.

The wind was dead against us from the South all the way down, and at last the boat-man took down the mizen sail. Oyster dredgers were at work, the men rowing their boats out into mid-stream pushing their oars with their faces to the bow, Venetian gondola fashion. The boat rope was fixed to an anchor at one end and a windlass on board at the other, and as the man rowed away from the anchor, the wheel flew round whirling and paid out as much rope as was wanted. Then the man worked the boat back to the anchor by the windlass and rope, scraping the oyster bank at the bottom meanwhile with his dredge. There used to be a great many oysters in the Fal. The river grew clearer and greener and at last we felt the swell of the sea, and the boat began to toss. Forests of sea weed and ore weed glided under water, and forests of ship masts from Falmouth Roads and Harbour loomed through the heat haze. The guard ship Ganges lay in the river, an old fashioned two decker with the tall elegant masts and tapering

21 HMS Ganges.

spars which one misses so much in the ironclads, and the long white bands checked with the black squares of the portholes. She has been here now some years and succeeded the St George as a training ship for boys. On board they are taught to make and do everything.

As we entered the Harbour the wind roughened and the boat pitched a little. It is a grand harbour, almost landlocked and looks as if it could hold all the navies of the world. In the middle of the Harbour lies the Black Rock, capped and marked by a sort of spire like an extinguisher. The Harbour has an unfinished look from the skeletons of docks, the pier piles &c which have never been completed and look sad and strange. Pendennis Castle on the height above at the Harbour mouth. Opposite to it St Mawes and Place, and on the headland beyond St Mawes, the white lighthouse of St Anthony.

22 Pendennis Castle at the mouth of the Fal.

We landed, and the boatman said he was not sorry to get to the end of his long pull. He could sail back easily. After a short walk up from the beach to the new Hotel, we went to the Station. Yesterday morning at 6 a.m. broad daylight there was a wreck in a dense fog on the Stags' Horns Rocks off the Lizard. The ship was from Odessa, 350 tons register, with 600 tons of wheat on board. All the crew, about 12, were saved, escaping in their boats just before the ship went down. They came to Falmouth last night and slept there, and this evening we found them all at Falmouth Station, departing to their several destinations. We spoke to some of them, and they told us about the wreck and their escape. Some of the crew were foreigners, Russians, perhaps, though they spoke English well. The Captain, a short man with a red face, was walking about in a white deerstalker. He looked very foreign and Russian and reminded me strongly of Captain Adam. A good-humoured looking man who was both second mate and boat-swain told us who was who. The first mate, a fiery, foreign-looking, black-haired, darkskinned little man with a blue slop, was in furious excitement and wrath and could not be pacified or comforted. The trouble was that the railway officials would not take his luggage which was overweight without being paid for it. The fiery little mate would not pay a farthing, and stormed away at the porters for wanting to surcharge a poor sailor for his ship-wrecked luggage, and threatening to put the case in the Mercantile Gazette. A young man in a white straw hat, white linen jacket and white canvass shoes went about from one to another trying to make peace. He was connected with the

Royal Cornwall Sailors' Home and intending son-in-law elect to an old man who was also trying to mediate. But all in vain. The luggage was left on the platform. The good-humoured boatswain's brow gradually grew blacker and blacker. At last the tempest burst in a volley of threats and abuse. The men and boys of the shipwrecked crew were bundled into another carriage and we moved away from the platform amid a storm of curses, from boatswain and mate, the porters remaining unmoved. I thought it seemed hard that the poor shipwrecked fellows should be surcharged for their bundles of clothes &c and the little they had saved from the wreck, even if it were a little overweight, and the case was a very peculiar one.

23 Carn Brea Castle.

Friends in Council.

At dinner we had some delicious red mullet which Mrs H. bought in Truro market this morning.

Thursday, 21 July

Breakfast 6.45. Mrs H. drove us in the pony carriage to Perranwell Station in time for the 7.35 train to Hayle. By train to Hayle passing Scorrier, Chace Water, Redruth &c and the old ruined castle on Carn Brea. The journey lay through a great mining district, chiefly tin. "Thou art Lord of the world, bright Tin" (Miners' Song). The bowels of the earth ripped open, turned inside out in the search for metal ore, the land defiled and cumbered with heaps and wastes of slag and rubbish, and the waters poisoned with tin and copper washings.

24 'a great mining district' ... Dolcoath.

The Cornish villages bare, bleak, barren and ugly, whitewashed and often unsheltered by a single tree, grouped or scattered about monotonous wastes.

Reached Hayle at 9. Walked through the ugly town, half seaport, half manufacture, and crossed a dreary creek by a bridge over which runs a tramway for coal &c. The tide was low and the wastes of sand and mud festered and sweltered in the hot sun. Some colliers and other vessels lay at the wharves and piers along the creek. From the Phillack shore we looked back upon the long irregular town, with its scattered rows of white houses and buildings straggling out into the country or up and down the creek, the masts of the vessels and the lofty black timber viaducts soaring over the streets with their long stilted legs. "Bal" (mine) girls and women walking about in huge white calico bonnets flapping over their faces.

We climbed over a gate at the foot of a hill close by the creek shore and climbed a steep path through a pretty wood, part of the grounds of La Rivière, to the mansion, a white square formal house. In the plantation was a path

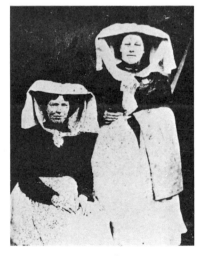

25 'Bal' women.

leading down to a celebrated well in a dark cool square chamber cut in the rock.

We went through a door in the wall into the fine granite-walled garden of La Rivière. A large fierce tall black dog was walking solemnly up and down curling his tail over his back, but a garden woman told us he would not hurt us. I especially admired the solid massive granite masonry of the garden wall.

Fruit, vegetables, flowers grew in profusion, everything very large, a fine lemon plant &c. Mrs H. gathered and gave me to eat some delicious red and green apples.

The gardener let us out of the sultry burning garden by the opposite door, through which the tall black dog seized the opportunity to escape and he could with difficulty be recovered. Up the steep narrow rocky lane or village street towards the Church of Phillack which grandly crowns the hill with its fine square pinnacled tower rising above the roofs of "Church Town", which straggle up the hill or group and gather round the Church. Immediately below, the Rectory nestles in pretty plantations and gardens. Miss Hockin was waiting breakfast for us and we fell to our second break-fast at 9.45 in a comfortable old-fashioned room with a most delightful deep bow window. Miss Hockin was alone in the house, her brother the Rector and his nieces being away on visits. After breakfast a curate came in from the Church where there had been a wedding, and just after the ceremony was over, the sextoness had informed him that the bride was the sister of the bridegroom's deceased wife.

Portraits on the dining room wall of H.'s fine-looking grandfather and grandmother.

Miss Hockin took us out into the garden and showed us the new croquet lawn, with

26 Phillack Rectory: watercolour by Miss Charlotte Hockin.

terraces and flights of steps with bright white stone balustrades leading down to the old kitchen garden. Against the hedge of the lower garden fern walk stood the white wooden figurehead of a ship, the image of a woman. Miss Hockin showed us her ferns and flower garden, stables and poultry and the playful brown and white setter Maida, who was almost beside herself with excitement and delight at seeing so many people, and longing to be loosed.

Next Mrs H., H. and I went into the Church. Just inside the lychgate there is as in many Cornish churchyards a large slab of granite, almost coffin-shaped, called the "resting stone". Here the bearers rest the coffin when waiting for the clergyman. A little further on stood a tall granite churchyard cross.

The Church has been nicely restored and has some fair stained glass. The choir sur-plices hung in the vestry. The Church stands very near the sea between the high white sand banks and the village. The tower must be a landmark, and the wind drives in so furiously sometimes from the N. coast that the clergyman can scarcely be heard utter-ing a sound for the violence and roaring of the storm.

Phillack Church is dedicated to St Felicitas. "Phillack" is said to be a corruption of "Felicitas". One stained window represents the slaughter of the children of St Felici-tas before her eyes.

From the Church we three went up over the sand "towans" or banks. Probably "to-wans" is the same word as "dunes".

These sand banks are high ridges of bright white sand, very fine and shifting. Coarse grass, rushes and thistles and a few sea plants grow about the "towans".

We walked along the top of a "hedge" as it is called in Cornwall, i.e. a turf topped stone wall, pretty broad. The fine shifting white sand was deep and loose. Seaward, the towans slope away down to a beautiful sweep of white sandy beach on the shore of the Atlantic. There was nothing but blue water between us and America. The sea was an intense deep blue, almost purple, and as we stood on the level shore seeming at moments to be nearly black. Then clouds came over the sun and the sea became deep dark green. This part of the coast is called Hayle Bay, a little bay within the larger bay of St Ives. Cliffs, coves and headlands stretched round the left sweep of the bay to the white cluster of houses, the town of St Ives within the point of the left horn of the bay. On the right the white towans trended round with the coast to the cliffs off which are the island and white lighthouse of Godrevy.

The breakers were singing and surfing over the rocks of Godrevy called the "Nine Maidens", and we could see in the distance the white fringe of foam which tells that the sea is too rough to admit of any one landing on the lighthouse island. About Godrevy and all along the North Coast there are a great many seals. Once at Godrevy the Hs. saw a fearful battle between a seal and a large conger eel. The seal had got his teeth in the conger and the conger had coiled his folds round the seal's neck and was trying to choke him. The seal kept on throwing up his head and trying to toss the conger up out of the water that he might have more power than the eel. It was a fierce and dreadful fight, but at last the seal killed the conger.

On the hill above St Ives stands up against the sky the column or obelisk set up by a St Ives man named Knill, who left a sum of money to be distributed among such of the maidens of St Ives who would go up to the hill on a certain day and dance round this pillar.

One must not talk much to St Ives men about hakes, or ask them "Who whipped the hake?"

The vicar of St Ives says, the smell of fish there is sometimes so terrific as to stop the church clock.

The tide had just turned and was ebbing, and a small herd of cows lay on the hard dry white sand just above high water mark. We picked up a number of pretty shells on the beach, and I meant to have taken them home, but unfortunately left them at Phillack Rectory.

We did not know it at the time, but while we were enjoying ourselves on the beach a poor miner who had gone out to bathe in his dinner hour was drowning in the bay very near us.

The sea fog came rolling up from the Atlantic in a dense purple bank, and the sea changed colour to a deep dark green. Returning to the Rectory over the high towans we got the first glimpse of the bristling pointed summit of St Michael's Mount, and could catch the North and South coasts looking from sea to sea and shore to shore

27 St Michael's Mount.

across the narrow neck of land or isthmus which divides the Cornwall of Cornwall-West Penwith from the rest of the county.

We passed a cottage whose front wall was entirely faced with shells large and small gathered on the shores of the bay. Unfortunately the shells had all been whitewashed over so that it was very difficult to make them out, or they would have been extremely pretty. It was a nice comfortable cottage with its back to the sea and a good garden in front.

Dinner at Phillack Rectory at 2. Ducks, green peas, grapes and other fruit which we brought with us &c. At 2.30 the carriage and nice pair of brown horses came to the door and Miss Hockin drove us through Hayle to Marazion or Market Jew as the old-fashioned folks still call it. We drove from one coast to the other, from the N. to the S. coast in about an hour. The horses were put up at Market Jew, an ugly barren-looking white-washed little town like many of the small Cornish towns, bare, dreary, monotonous and utterly uninteresting in everything except its name and the legends that cluster about the place. The tide was out and we walked across to St Michael's Mount, about a quarter of a mile over a narrow spit of wet sand, mud and shingle, slippery rocks and seaweed, and jumping over the little pools left by the ebbing tide. At high tide this spit of land is entirely covered, and the Mount becomes an island.

28 'A winding walk ... leads ... to the battery platforms'.

At the foot of the Mount is a graveyard enclosed by a wall, but there is no Church or Chapel there. The Chapel is in the Castle on the crest of the Mount. Round the graveyard cluster a few white-washed cottages and the outbuildings and premises of the Castle. A winding walk among granite rocks and crags and remnants of ruined walls strewn about the green turf leads up the steep conical Mount to the battery platforms and embrasures where several small cannon are planted. There was a party of people on the highest battlements of the square Castle tower, and from below we watched a gentleman getting cautiously over the battlements and letting himself down slowly into the seat of St Michael's Chair, a little stone hollow in the outside of the turret,

29 View from St Michael's Mount to Marazion.

which forms a seat slightly hollowed, with the turret behind to lean the back against, while the legs of the occupant dangle in the air into space at a ghastly height above the rocks and roofs below. It is more difficult to get out of the Chair than to get into it, as the legs have to be drawn and curled up on to the seat of the Chair before the sitter can rise.

The Chair is supposed to have formed the stone cresset in which the famous Beacon of St Michael's Mount used to be lighted.

"High on St Michael's Mount it shone".

30 St Michael's Chair.

Leaving the two ladies gathering ferns about the rocks, H. and I went up into the Castle, up the corkscrew stair on to the top of the tower, and I sat in St Michael's Chair. From the Castle roof there is a splendid view of Mount's Bay. The sea was as blue as sapphire. On the right horn of the bay lay Penzance (Pen Sans, the Holy Headland) sweltering white in the burning sun. On the left the coast trended away cape after cape towards the Lizard Point. Behind lay white Marazion blazing in the heat, and the flat sandy land amongst salt marshes, creeks and lagoons.

We descended from the Castle tower into the Chapel, which is seldom used except when one of the family in Orders is staying at the Mount. The Chapel is small, but very pretty and simply furnished. Under one of the stalls in the choir is a trap door and stone staircase of a few steps, the only entrance to a small round dungeon chamber hewn in the living rock. We were given a broad candlestick by the pretty delicate gentle melancholy girl who showed us over the Castle, and descended into this dungeon through the narrow trap door. The skeleton of a man was found here some time ago. Coming up the steps again H. who was carrying the candle turned round, as he was emerging through the trap door, to show the steps with the light, and bruised his hip severely against the corner of a beam.

31 The Chapel.

The Castle is very small but a perfect little gem. There is the portcullis, the guard room &c, and everything complete.

32 The Chevy Chace Room.

The dining hall is a fine room with a beautiful timber open-work roof. All round the walls and cornices are carvings of scenes in Chevy Chace, whence it is called the Chevy Chace Room. The drawing rooms are smaller but very pretty and picturesque with beautiful views out over sea. Some of the family had just arrived, and it was doubtful if we could be shown the dwelling rooms. The girl went cautiously first and peeped into the rooms to see if any one were there before she admitted us. On the drawing room table lay a gentleman's hat and a telescope, evidently lately laid there, but we encountered no one. In the guard room were some specimens of old arms, cross bows, swords, guns, cuirasses &c.

The signatures of the Queen, Prince Consort and some of the Royal Family, Prince and Princess of Wales, suite &c were framed and glazed with the pens used in writing the signatures. The Princess of Wales slept here two nights. A brass plate was let into the rock where the Queen stepped on land at the Mount.

A man was bathing in the bay, plunging from a boat – enviable – for the heat on the rocks on the sunny side of the Mount was intense. I should like to see a great storm from St Michael's Mount. The worst storms on these coasts are generally in February.

We had some trouble to find the ladies, who were searching for ferns along the lower rocks, and had found some Asplenium Marinum and Asplenium Lanceolatum. These ferns grow in the narrowest crevices of the rocks and it is very hard to get them up by the root. We made a tour of the Mount, looking up at the house founded upon a rock, the batteries, the Castle tower, the Chapel window &c, and then walked back across the narrow spit of rock and shingle, mud, sand and seaweed to Market Jew. The horses were immediately put to, and we drove to Hayle Station and came back to Perranwell by train. It was curious that though directly we left Phillack the whole of the North Coast was wrapped in a dense sea fog, the South Coast only 8 miles away remained bright, clear and sunny golden all the afternoon. Tamarisks grew in profusion in the hedges, on the walls, in the cottage gardens and all along the road sides. They look something like fennel, or asparagus, and still more like cypress.

Today was the Confirmation at Hay, and I thought of the Clyro young people.

Friday, 22 July

Miss Emily and Miss Charlotte Hockin came from Truro to breakfast at 8.30. At 9.30 we all started to drive to Mullion in a nice roomy waggonette, large enough to carry 10 people, drawn by a pair of gallant greys. Drove through St Stithians to Gweek where we stopped to lunch by a hedge-side and brook while one of the horses, who had cast a shoe just before, was being shod. A pretty road through woods and fields and across one or two trout streams, but still through a mining country, the mine stacks, works and chimneys rising white on every hill.

On through the pretty woods of Trelowarren Park, which Sir Richard Vivian kindly lets people drive through from lodge to lodge. Soon after this we got into the Serpentine district. The roads were made of marble, black marble, the dust of which

33 Mullion Church.

looked like coal dust. The country became very wild and timber almost disappeared. Along the roadsides grew large bushes three and four feet high of beautiful heaths, white, pink and rose colour, growing as freely as gorse grows with us. We stopped the carriage and gathered some fine sprays. The splendour and luxuriance of the heather, I never saw anything like this before. The strong square tower of Mullion Church stood up before us against the sky on the hill top as we mounted the last rise, and then the glimpse of the bay and the broad blue Cornish sea. Drove through the village to the Old Inn, kept by Mary Mundy a genuine Cornish Celt, and a good specimen of one, impulsive, warm-hearted, excitable, demonstrative, imaginative, eloquent.

We went into a sitting room upstairs, unpacked the hampers and ordered dinner to be ready when we came back in an hour's time. The sitting room was over the stable and we heard the horses stamping underneath. The window looked out over a waving field of reddening wheat which grew close up to the cottage wall, and the swaying ears of which were not far below the window sill.

34 'The seats ... curiously carved'.

We went to the Church first. The massive tower which serves as a landmark is made of great square blocks of dark grey granite. The white lines and seams of mortar show conspicuously against the blackish grey stone. The granite is so hard that it wears little with the weather, and there is not the crumbling venerable look of age about some of these churches which one usually sees in an old building. All is hard, sharp and clear. A good lychgate, and the Church has been nicely restored, plenty of space, not over-crowded with pews, broad open aisles and choir and no altar rails. The seats are very remarkable, very old, low-backed and open (showing that the modern seats are only the ancient ones revived), made of dark oak almost black and very massive, and most curiously carved into quaint grotesque representations of Scripture history, a perfect study in themselves and an epitome of the Bible carven in oak.

We went to the Rectory for a few minutes to call for the Miss Hockins, and then walked down to Mullion Cove by the lifeboat shed, along a lane and through wheatfields gay with red poppies, blue cornflowers and yellow Lady's Finger.

At the Cove we parted from the ladies, leaving them to sit on the rocks and sketch and return at their leisure. H. and I went up a winding path on to the cliffs on the other side of the Cove, passing some cottages and fishing outbuildings, net houses, boat houses &c. On the wall of one was nailed an immense and hideous skate.
The view of Mullion Cove from the cliff is very beautiful. The deep blue sea rippling into the deep small cove shut in by the great dark cliffs, the fringe of white foam along the rocks. At the foot of the cliffs, the streaks and patches of deep brilliant intense emerald green "playing" into blue where the white sand beneath ended, and the rocks or beds of dark seaweed began, the black caves in the rocks, the dark rocky island guarding the mouth of the Cove, the fishing boats drawn up on the white shingle beach, the pilot boat with her red brown sails at anchor outside, the "Gull Rock" with the white gulls sitting on it or gliding out from their nests in its dark recesses and float-

35 Mullion Cove: watercolour by Miss Charlotte Hockin.

ing over the blue water with a mournful wild cry, the cormorants black and evil-look-ing basking on the sunny rocks, flapping their wings and spreading them to dry or flying slowly and heavily from cliff to cliff.

We walked along the edge of the high sheer cliffs to the Cathedral Rock with its towers, walls and shafts covered with a rich growth of grey, green, and bright golden and orange lichens. Ferns grew in the crevices and the turf was enamelled with flowers, pimpernel &c. We climbed upon the Rock and looked down the sheer wall into the blue sea foaming at the foot of the cliff. Upon the top of the cliff was a signal house, flagstaff and mortar for firing ropes over wrecked ships.

We descended off the cliff on to the fine white sand of the beautiful little Polurrian Bay beach. The tide had just turned and was ebbing. Broken cuttle fish lay about on the sand, and two black cormorants flew overhead going inland like two devils. The sea was very calm but a slight roar resounded from the echoing cliffs as the waves broke in the hollow bay. There were no shells on the sand, the sea is too rough and

36 *Kynance Cove.*

breaks them into pieces. As we went up from Pollurian Beach to Mullion we passed a farmyard in which were some large long-horned cows, of a curious light bay colour. They were Spanish cattle. There are a great many of these cattle in this part of Cornwall.

The ladies had not come in when we returned to the Old Inn, and we had to wait dinner for them a long time. At length they appeared scarlet and almost exhausted, for the heat was tremendous and they had followed us over the cliffs, finishing up by losing the way, struggling across country over fences and through standing corn. They were almost too much exhausted to eat, and we were delayed until late in the afternoon.

At last we got off and drove to Kynance Cove. The carriage was left on the moor (or "croft" as it is called here) above, and we scrambled down into the Cove. The tide was ebbing fast and it was nearly low water. We wandered about through the Dining Room and Drawing Room Caves, and among the huge serpentine cliffs and the vast detached rocks which stand like giants guarding the Cove. I never saw anything like the wonderful colour of the serpentine rocks, rich, deep, warm, variegated, mottled and streaked and veined with red, green and white, huge blocks and masses of precious stone, marble on every side, an enchanted cove, the palace of the Nereids.

The retreating tide lapped against the feet of the marble cliffs, stirring and lifting the long seaweed about the rocks. The sun was sinking behind the vast rock called the Asparagus Island. Round the dark rock edges brightened the aureole, and the light came softened and mellowed into the Cove. Between the guardian giant rocks, spaces of deep blue rippling sea, and white sails disappearing behind one rock and emerging again to pass behind another. The splendour of the place, the gorgeous blue and beauty of the broad sea, the coloured rocks, the towering cliffs, the coast, the golden swimming mellow light amongst the huge dark rock masses, indescribable.

We gathered some seaweed off the rocks to take home for a weather gage, and H. knocked off the cliff a piece of serpentine rock for me to bring away as a remembrance of the place and a specimen of the rocks. He described it as having been "struck off by the hoof of the learned Erasmus". I made an attempt to get to the "Bellows", a funnel hole in the rocks through which the sea rushes up with great violence in certain states of the weather and tide, but the tide had not ebbed far enough. I got round one point, but the wet marble rocks were as slippery as ice, and in trying to climb them I only slipped and fell with my feet in the water.

    We brought away some remembrances of the place from the stands of serpentine brooches, bracelets, whistles &c kept by women at the Cove. Some of the candlesticks &c were very beautiful.

37 Landewednack Church and Church-Town.

Leaving Kynance Cove we drove on to the Lizard, through a wild strange treeless district which would have been a wilderness but for the crops of low corn divided by "hedges", i.e. turf-topped walls with walks along the top. A small bare hamlet here and there or a group of white houses, and lone church towers rising over the desolate flats – (Ruan Major, Ruan Minor, Landewednack etc).

The long straight white road stretched away over the moors towards the sea among the granite and heath, granite and heath, heath and granite, heath and granite.

We put up the horses at the cluster of white houses that make Lizard Town. The ladies staid at the inn while H. and I walked down to the Point. The two great twin white lighthouses standing on the Point looking always out to sea. They are connected by a range of low buildings, all the walls and everything intensely white, glaring white. The blue sea rippled softly against the foot of the wild broken cliff that sweeps curving up into the noble headland. At the base of the Point the cliff is scooped into wild fantastic caves and shapes, and a strange ruin of rocks lies broken in scattered confusion along the fringe of shore. A little way from the Point rises a low long line of black broken jagged teeth of cruel rocks, called the Stags' Horns. This was where the wheat ship struck last Tuesday and there were her top masts standing up a little above the water at low tide, with a red flag still flying.

We had not time to explore the interior of the lighthouse, but we walked round it and through one of the courtyards below the white high towers. A barque was standing in very close to the Point to make a tack up Channel, so close that it almost seemed as if she would run ashore on the Stags' Horns. Then a pilot boat shot out of a bay. White, brown and dark grey sails flying up and down the Channel. Gulls were wheeling and sweeping, white with long curving wings against the dark cliffs. The sea was smooth and only seemed to quiver and shimmer, but now and then a spirt of foam shot up from a black rock and fell back in spray.

We went back to the inn and joined the ladies at tea, and then went out to look at the serpentine shops and bought some more remembrances. It is said that the Lizard people are of Spanish descent, and certainly we did see one or two peculiarly swarthy blackhaired people. As we drove away from the Lizard the sun was setting on the horizon of the wide desolate plain, and making all round the West and North a "low splendour" in a cloudless sky. The night was deliciously cool and the light faded very gradually as we drove home.

The red flames burst and roared from the tops of the tall mine chimneys. We reached Tullimaar at 11 p.m., and before the gallant greys reached their stable in Falmouth, they had travelled 50 miles.

38 'The two great twin white lighthouses'.

39 'Gulls ... white against the dark cliffs'.

In one of the serpentine shops at the Lizard there was a stuffed Cornish Chough. He is an elegantly-shaped black bird cleanly made with red or orange beak and legs. He is very rarely found now even along the Cornish cliffs.

Saturday, 23 July

Last night the owls were hooting loud and fast across the creek from the woods of Carclew, and the harriers bayed from the Carclew kennels as if they were famished. Walked round the grounds with H., and saw the ruins of the old harrier kennels in the plantation. There is a white bulldog with one black cheek and ear named Bob, chained in the stable yard. H. has a house full of rabbit hutches in which are fine lop-eared rabbits. We found two of the young rabbits dead this morning.

Miss Emily Hockin insisted on being driven home to Truro last night after we came home at 11, though it is a 5 miles drive, and she had a bed offered her and it was very inconvenient to send a man out. She did not reach home till after midnight.

Miss Charlotte stayed till the 4 o'clock train today. Before dinner we had two games of croquet, she and H. against Mrs H. and myself, and we each won a game. In the evening we were walking in the grounds. H. said "Do you hear that noise like a cough?" It was a deer in Carclew Park across the creek calling to her fawn. At the same time a strange bird was trilling in a low key.

There is a pretty walk above the creek, called the "Shady Walk", which Dora admired very much.

"I know a bank whereon the wild thyme grows".

Mrs H. has two pet toads, which live together in a deep hole in the bottom of a stump of an old tree. She feeds them with bread crumbs when they are at home, and they make a funny little plaintive squeaking noise when she calls them. Sometimes they are from home, especially in the evenings.

40 Carclew.

In the kitchen live a pair of doves in a large cage, and the house is filled with their soft sweet deep cooing.

Near the Falmouth Lodge in a deep cool walk above the road, there is a pretty oval pond, wire-fenced round, containing rocks, ferns, water-lilies and goldfish. It is so entirely surrounded and overhung with trees that it is quite hidden till you come close to it, and you pass along the drive above within a few feet of the fishpond without suspecting its existence. A horizontal shaft like the adit of a mine pierces the bank above the pond, and runs up under the lawn &c to the springs which supply the house and garden pumps. Through this adit these springs supply the fishpond.

Sunday, 24 July

We went to Church twice, morning and evening, at 11 and 6.30. The way to Church is very pleasant, up the shrubbery, through a flower garden and by a greenhouse, into outer kitchen gardens, then across the back lane by a private walk through private doors into the churchyard. The Church has a fine old ivy-grown tower with pinnacles, and a noble high flight of many broad granite steps leads up to the churchyard gate. The Chancel is restored, the nave &c still church-warden's Gothic. There is a very nice pretty pulpit hanging which Mrs H. made and gave. Very few people in Church. The heat excessive. The clergyman, Mr Hawkins, read some parts of the service very fast, much too fast, especially the Litany, but preached a good sermon.

The privacy, quietness and deep peacefulness of this place is very delightful, particularly on Sundays.

In the afternoon we had coffee out in the summer house and sat there talking till the heat of the day had abated. "Aside the devil turned &c &c – " Ah, how intelligible.

In the evening we went to Church again at 6.30. As we left Church the clergyman rushed out after us in his cassock. Mrs H. and I had gone on before, but he button-holed H. and proposed calling on me tomorrow. To my great relief H. rather discouraged his intentions than otherwise, by saying that he would not find us at home as we should be touring about all the week.

As we came in from Church it was growing dusk, and a fern owl flew over the lawn.

In the farmhouse yard between Tullimaar and the Vicarage there stands a great high picturesque old draw well, approached by stone steps round the well.

The front of the gardener's house at Tullimaar is covered by a superb Wisteria, which is just beginning to blossom a second time.

Monday, 25 July. St James' Day

Emily's wedding day.

Lounging on the lawn all the morning on the garden seat under the ilex oak reading books and papers, especially Bottrell's (the old Celt's) book of Cornish legends. I find many words, ideas and superstitions and customs kindred to those of Wales.

The deer across the creek calling their fawns in Carclew Park.

41 Fore Street, Redruth.

Late in the morning an expedition was arranged to Portreath on the North coast, and Martin the groom was sent into Falmouth with the mare Lily to bring back a double dogcart. We started after dinner, driving through Redruth, a dreary uninteresting money-making place in the heart of the mining district.

A swift narrow stream of water red with tin came rushing down a hill from a mine.

One must not talk to a Redruth man about "Redruth Kings", or ask him "Who crowned the donkey?" because on the coronation day of one of the English Kings the good people of Redruth crowned a donkey and paraded him round the town, and this has been a joke and reproach against them ever since.

We put up at the inn at Portreath and walked up on to the grand cliffs covered with heather, purple to the very edge. The blue Atlantic lay at our feet far below, breaking at the feet of the sheer cliffs and stretching away to the New World. On the left the rocky iron-bound coast trended round to Godrevy white lighthouse on the rocky island, and St Ives.

On the right the great cliffs rose sheer from the blue sea and stood away cape beyond cape, headland after headland, towards St Agnes Head till lost in the dim blue haze. The tide was ebbing, and at the base of the cliffs the waves leaped and ran up their sides in jets and spirts of white foam and spray, falling back again baffled from off the black slippery rocks. Sea gulls floated and swept wheeling midway down the cliffs, and some were swimming and paddling like ducks in the quiet water of the little coves, riding easily and happily on the gentle swell.

We went down a steep path to the edge of some rocks overlooking a small cove and then, leaving Mrs H. sitting on the turf, H. and I clambered down a rough zig-zag track among the rocks and jumped down on to the sands of the cove. A little waterfall leapt from the cliff edge above, and fell into the middle of the cove in a drenching shower of large drops on sand and shingle. A cave lay back in the rocks at the bend of the cove, and a luxuriant forest of ferns draped the rock with a green curtain overhead and out of reach.

In these cliffs along the North coast are many seal "sawns" (caves, holes).

In one of the great caves among the cliffs of Portreath abode the Giant Wrath, who waded after ships passing by and pulled them into his cavern, and sunk those out of wading depth by slinging rocks at them. (See Bottrell's Cornish Tales).

H. climbed about the rocks as light and active as a kid, while I lumbered after him as clumsy as an elephant. Once down in the cove I had the greatest difficulty in climbing up again on to the narrow rock ledge whence we had jumped down into the cove, a little rock wall only 8 or 9 feet deep, while H. was up in a moment with a hop, step and jump.

42 Portreath Harbour.

My awkwardness delayed us some time, and when we reached the top of the rocks we found Mrs H. still sitting on the turf waiting patiently for us, but wondering what had become of us and whether we meant to take up our abode in the cove for the remainder of the term of our natural lives.

Coming back towards Portreath we went down into the bay where the Red River runs into the sea in twenty narrow shallow arms, staining the sea red all round the bay. The tide was just gone out far enough to let us go through a tunnel in the cliff into another little bay with some pretty coves beyond, where some boys were bathing. The sea was very beautiful, rougher than I have seen it yet at all on this coast, and so fascinating that it was difficult to tear one's-self away from the last sight of the waves and cliffs and rocks and foam.

The touching, deeply affecting story of the gallantry of the St Ives lifeboat men.

We went back to the inn to tea and after tea, leaving Mrs H. at the inn, H. and I walked down through the coal wharves by the moored colliers to the pier end. Presently a young man joined us pointing out an object that he thought was a seal. The thing disappeared, reappeared, came nearer, and it *was* a seal diving and fishing off the rocks. H. saw it very plainly. There was no doubt about its being a seal. It rose so near, once, that its teeth could almost be seen. I was sorry I could not see it, I should like to have seen a seal.

It was growing dusk as we got back to the inn. The carriage was ready and we started about eight. The white-footed mare brought us back in splendid style, up and down hill, but when she got home her shoulder was wrung by a badly fitting collar and a sharp seam in the leather. The sky had darkened all round as if from a storm, but overhead there was a grand break in the clouds, lurid with a deep copper thundery tinge.

Tuesday, 26 July

Drove to Falmouth at noon with Lily in the double dogcart, and blinding clouds and storms of dust raised by little whirlwinds. A fresh breeze roughened the Harbour, and the Roads were full of white horses careering in from the sea.

The town was very lively by reason of the Regatta, stirring music of fifes and drums, all the Falmouth people out upon the narrow winding streets in their best clothes and gayest colours, the streets thronged with crowds marching along with the fifes and drums, and the town crier, a tall greybeard man in semi-uniform and high hat, stalked in solemn majesty with his bell, making proclamation that [at] 1, 3, 5, and 7 o'clock the steam boat Pendennis would make the tour of the Harbour, taking people to see the Regatta and the different points of interest round the Harbour. We meant to have taken boat and rowed across the Harbour to Place to see the pretty chapel, but the sea was too rough for comfort, and besides there was hardly time as we had to leave Falmouth again by train soon after 4.

There were all sorts of races but the great event of the day was a fine race between four pilot boats, Nos. 13, 3, 10, 5. They started from the Committee boat, went out of the Harbour far out to sea, round two boats moored and then home, passing in and out through the shipping and round the man-of-war guardship Ganges. It was a first rate race, and the two leading boats No. 13 and No. 3 started well and got away very close to each other. No. 13 tore along through the water under every stitch of canvass she could hold, heeling over and the sea boiling and foaming past her bows as she flew. No. 3 was pressing close upon her, coming up hand over hand as if she meant to take the wind out of her rival's sails. It was beautiful to see the boats straining every nerve as if they had life, now one gaining, now the other, as each of the fine vessels tried all she knew to win. They had been over the course once, and were just sweeping through the shipping in the Roads and gliding out of the Harbour for the second round when at a critical moment as No. 3 seemed to be gaining, her peak halyards

43 Pendennis Castle.

snapped and down came her top sail. A groan of pity and disappointment ran through the excited people who lined the cliffs as they saw the accident. No. 13 instantly sprang ahead, though No. 3 recovered herself gallantly in the third and last round. She never quite made up her lost ground and came in second. She got the first prize though, we heard afterwards, because she was a smaller boat than No. 13. No. 10 was third and No. 5 last. They both sailed well these two last boats, but they were never in the race for first or second places, they only steadily kept their distance.

It happened fortunately that the race was over just in time for us to see the finish, as the leading boat glided past the goal and the gun was fired, the white puff of smoke almost clearing away from the Committee boat before we heard the boom of the gun across the Harbour.

Crowds of people were gathered black in lines and masses along the rails that guard the edge of the cliff, and crowds were strolling about the roads and walks round Pendennis Castle, and sitting on the dry dusty turf slopes beneath the Castle which command a view of the Harbour and the bay. We went up to the Castle and walked round the battlements where two long guns are mounted pointing across bay and Harbour, and pyramids of shot rest on the turf behind them. The Castle consists chiefly of the fort and a Governor's house in which is still shown the room in which Prince Charles, afterwards Charles II, was concealed.

We got back from Falmouth by train at 4.30. Walked from Perranwell Station to Tullimaar, and on the way H. took me to see a place where Osmundas grow luxuriantly along the banks and hedges and in the ditches. They were growing like weeds, magnificent plants, some nearly six feet high, but so common about here as to be quite valueless and unregarded. Amongst the Osmundas and brambles H. pointed out a little round pool, overgrown and almost encircled with tangled briars, St Perran's well, a common-looking place, dark and muddy as if cattle had been trampling in the water.

We came in by the fishpond and lower walk. From this walk there is a beautiful evening view up the creek when the sun is shining as it was this afternoon, Goon Vrea mansion bosomed in its woods above the creek, Carclew Park and woods sloping down to the water's edge, the cottages beneath the dark woods, nestling by the creek shore, with their blue hazy smoke curling up into the evening sunlight, and blue hills rising beyond above the head of the creek, the flashing of the water and the top of the tall foundry chimneys rising above the trees.

Preparing for the grand expedition to the Land's End tomorrow. Mrs H. let me come into the kitchen and help to pack the hampers. Three candles were burning on the kitchen table, and the cook said that the person who was nearest to the shortest candle would be married first. Some people put it "Will die first". It seems to be an old saying about three lighted candles together, but it was quite new to me.

A visit to the cellars, &c. I cannot say that I rendered any very material assistance, but we were encouraged on this and other occasions as follows, "Come friends, &c" or "Now my lords and gentlemen, if you want to know what I am doing, it is, so and so, &c".

Wednesday, 27 July

To the Land's End. Early breakfast at 7, and desperate rush to 7.35 train at Perranwell, Mrs H. driving in the pony carriage, H. and I running the short cut by the Church for bare life like rabbits. Caught the Truro train by one minute. From Truro to Penzance

44 A waggonette on the Penzance – Land's End road.

by rail. Capt. and Mrs Parker and Miss Lewis got in at Camborne from Rosewarne to join the picnic. By the time we reached Penzance, I was becoming rather cooler. St Michael's Mount in mist and the sea very smooth. H. had telegraphed to the Western Hotel, Penzance, for a carriage and pair, and we were met at the station by a small waggonette with a bay and grey. With some difficulty we stowed all the hampers on board and set off, driving along the beach for some distance till we turned inland by the Church of [St Peter] and along the pretty road to the cross made by the meeting of the four beautiful avenues. A little further on an oak arched completely over the road, and the driver Edward Noy said that no other oak arched the road between this place and London.

A short rude stone cross, plainly extremely ancient, stood on a pedestal in a little niche in the bank by the road side. The driver said it was called a "Saxon Cross".

45 'An oak arched completely over the road'.

46 'A short rude stone cross'.

There were some long steep hills on the road, but the horses in perfect training took us up and down capitally. Capt. Parker was the life of the party and kept the waggonette in a roar. Egg sandwiches went round, and presently we stopped to have sherry all round.

When we were ready to go on, Capt. Parker said to Mrs H., "If you wanted a donkey to go on what would you say?" Then he added instantly in a loud voice, "Proceed Edward". There was a roar from the waggonette. Everyone was convulsed, and Edward grinned a tremendous grin, looked somewhat red and foolish, and *proceeded* amidst a storm of laughter. It was a very merry party.

The Scilly telegraph wire accompanied us along the road.

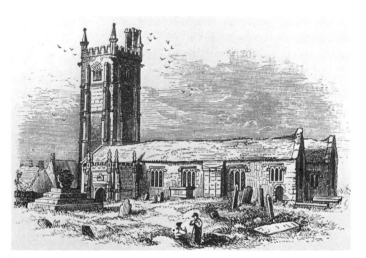

47 St Buryan Church.

The first striking object was the great tower of Buryan Church, very massive and lofty, and used as a landmark and a beacon tower. Through the bare straggling village of Buryan, and then a glimpse of blue sea down a gorge between two high hills, and a bold headland standing out into the sea, which I in my simplicity, and all on the alert to catch sight of the famous Point, immediately set down as being the Land's End. But the Land's End was yet a long way off. Down one tremendous hill and up another, and we came to a strange bare wild village where everything was made of granite – cottages, walls, roofs, pigs "crows" (sties), sheds, outbuildings, nothing but granite, enormous slabs of granite set up on end and roofed with other slabs.

The horses were put up at the inn, and we walked down first by field paths and stiles and then by a narrow pass cut in the cliffs and over steep slippery rock slopes and ledges to the Logan Stone. There is a considerable descent towards the sea before you get to the Logan Stone. It stands upon a lower range of cliffs almost overhanging the sea, and you do not see it before you come very near it.

We stopped on the way to wonder at the magnificent colour of the sea, the deep intense marvellous blue, waved and streaked with lines and patches of purest deepest softest green. Under one cliff in particular there was one spot, as if it were a round pool of green, brilliant as an emerald, and all the colour was intensified by the fringe of white foam where the water, though so calm, yet fretted against the base of the cliff.

The deep splendid blue too was deepened by contrast as the rippling ultramarine washed in upon the brilliant white sand of a little gem of a bay called [Porth Curnow], a nook or niche in the vast cliff wall. The water was so exquisitely clear down to its blue depths that from the cliffs high above we could see brown shoals of fish gliding about the rocks.

At the foot of the steep rock on which the Logan Stone is balanced a man stood ready to show the way up, and when he saw me coming he began to run up just like a monkey. His action was so sudden, strange and wild, and so exactly that of a monkey clambering up the bars of his cage, that I looked to see whether he had a tail. He helped me up capitally with knee and hand. I could never have got up by myself, for the rock faces were very steep, smooth and slippery. The guide wanted to put me up on to the top of the Logan Stone but I declined. He showed me the cleft in the cliff into which the Logan Stone rolled when Lieutenant

48 The Logan Rock.

Goldsmith and his crew upset it. The guide first put his shoulder under the Stone and rocked it, and then I did the same. It rocks perceptibly, though very slightly. But it has never rocked so well and easily since it was wilfully thrown down. The perfect balance of Nature could never be restored.

I found the rest of the party waiting for me, sitting on the opposite rock. An elderly grizzled man in a blue slop was offering photographs for sale. He was a boy when the Logan Stone was upset 46 years ago, and he remembered its being replaced.

As we returned up the narrow steep pass or gangway among the broken tumbled piles and wildernesses of rocks, H. and Captain Parker discovered the black streak of a vein or lode of tin in the rocky pathway under foot. The close solid black ore glittered and sparkled with a thousand tiny points, and I brought away a bit in remembrance of the place.

As we returned to the wild granite village along the field paths, a rude vulgar crew of tourists (real British) passed us going down to the cliffs, grinning like dogs, and one of the male beasts said in a loud insolent voice evidently meant for us to hear, "I hope they haven't upset the Logan Rock". For the moment I devoutly wished that we had.

The village was a paradise of black pigs which lay about in the glare of the sun under the hot granite walls, par-roasted but in great content.

At the inn we had some ale and cider, the horses were put to and we drove on to the nearest point to Tol-pedn-penwith which we could reach by carriage. Here H., Captain P. and I alighted, waved adieu to the ladies who drove on to the Land's End while we walked to the same point along the coast and over the line of magnificent cliffs and headlands which stand between.

Down a steep bank into a valley planted with potatoes and up a sharp rise over walls, peat, heather and granite boulders, and on the top of the moor the first things we saw were "the Landmarks", a white and black wall and tower surmounting it, and a conical red extinguisher a little nearer the sea.

A little further on we came upon the Funnel Rock, a vast funnel pit ending in a cave open to the sea, which roars up at high tide to the bottom of the Funnel and rushes up its sides. At low water this cavern can be entered from the beach and the bottom of the Funnel may be reached, but it is a perilous adventure, for if the rising tide catches the adventurer in this fearful trap there is small hope of escape. A young man was once caught in this way by the tide, but he managed to make someone hear and was drawn up just in time by ropes or clothes tied together.

49 The Cavern, Tol-Pedn.

Close by the Funnel Rock is the great rock, jutting out into the sea, called Tol-pedn-penwith, but the cliffs on either side are so magnificent that we could not certainly identify the point.

It was a grand walk and I should have been deeply sorry to have missed it. The only drawback was that Mrs H. was not with us. How she would have enjoyed that superb range of headlands and those cliffs rising sheer from the ocean, rearing themselves aloft in wild fantastic masses and strange awful shapes, the iron granite rocks split, riven, wrenched, torn asunder, tossed and tumbled in huge piles and vast fragments, some pieces of cliff leaning back, some tumbling forward, overhanging, tottering over the sea, as if they would plunge at any moment and nothing to show why they should not crash forward into the sea like falling towers, huge pinnacles and rocks like castle walls, rocking, staggering, leaning up against each other, precipices broken, ruined, undermined with caverns, the cliffs pierced and cleft by horrible chasm and abyss, deep narrow fissures and crevices in which the waves wash boiling, foaming, wearing the granite away gradually and threatening to detach large masses of rock from the mainland.

The incessant cry of the gulls and seamews wheeling about the cliffs and caves, and the cormorants fishing, or sitting on the rocks in the sun to dry.

Looking back and forward, there was the "endless range" of headlands, "cape beyond cape" fading dim blue into the great distance, and the intense blue boundless sea and the eternal white foam fringe at the foot of the cliffs.

On the horizon the Lighthouse on the Wolf Rock stood up like a tiny stick. Nearer shore rode the bell buoy, but we could not hear the solemn incessant tolling of the bell.

We saw the Ladder Rock and the Dollar Rock where a ship of the Spanish Armada was wrecked, dashed into the narrow chasm which separates the island rock from the main cliffs, and where the divers fished up part of her treasure of dollars sunk round the rock.

We were guided by Capt. P. to another Logan Rock smaller than the famous one but much more perfectly balanced and easily "logged" because it has never been disturbed. It could be easily rocked with one hand and would crack a nut. A child might move it.

There are several Logan Stones of various sizes, half a dozen at least. Our driver knew of six, and said the best was at Zennor, which can be rocked ("logged") with the thumb while two or three people are on the stone.

50 The Irish Lady.

There is another peculiar rock, called the "Irish Lady".

I was particularly struck by the magnificence of the lichens, especially the green mosses which fringe and drape the lee side of the cliffs and rocks. Some of the rock faces are thickly clothed and draped from top to bottom with these long deep luxuriant grey green and hoary fringes, relieved here and there by brilliant orange and yellow.

Samphire and Asplenium Marinum grow everywhere about the ledges and crevices of these cliffs.

We saw the great cavern called "Sawn Pyg".

H. and Capt. P. spied a young sparrow hawk and scrambled after it down the rocks, but it flew out on to an inaccessible ledge. Then in a deep hollow we came upon an old tin-stamping wheel and works on a small stream, disused, deserted, and looking so wild and strange that it might have belonged to and been worked by one of the old giants of the Land's End.

Not far off was the Telegraph House where the Scilly Cable leaves the mainland.

On the top of a hill crossing the moor was a gigantic wall in which was a gigantic stile. The wall was very high, and built dry with such enormous stones beautifully and regularly piled upon each other that it looked like an ancient wall made by the old Cornish giants.

Further on two men were lying on the turf by a broken wall, and a brown dog sprang on to the wall and barked wildly at us, while the men told us the way to the "First and

Last House". Crossing the croft near the Inn, while gathering heath Capt. P. killed a snake or viper with his stick, ripped it open with his knife and found three young mice inside. Edward Noy came to meet us, saying the ladies were waiting for us down among the rocks. And sure enough they were waiting and had been waiting for an hour or more. Famished they were, and some of them sleeping for hunger.

The Inn and a tent outside the house were occupied by a large vulgar picnic party, so we had our nice dinner among the rocks in aristocratic simplicity and seclusion. A "duke" is truly a lordly dish.

I was told that the wind here at times is so furious that four men have been wanted to take a lady out of her carriage and carry her into the Inn. Two young men have been needed to take an old man to his work, supporting him one on each side against the wind. A carriage has been lifted up into the air by the wind with its wheels whirling round. The panels and windows of a carriage have been so cut and scratched by the granite dust and sand (which when blown by the wind cuts and scores like diamond dust), that the carriage has had to be repainted and the windows replaced, because they were so scratched that it was impossible to see through them. Sometimes the Inn windows have to be barricaded as if a storm of rifle balls was expected.

After dinner Capt. P. took Miss Lewis and me down to the Land's End, a little triangular point of rock reached by passing round to the seaward side of a tall upright shaft of cliff. The accomplishment of an old dream.

The rocks at the Land's End are lower than the cliffs on either side, and they eventually run out into the sea below the triangular standing place in a low broken range or reef. But they are very strangely fantastically shaped, and some of them are exactly like long thin squared baulks of timber reared up and leaning against each other. One thing was wanting, a rougher sea. The sea was very calm. But had the water been broken we should have missed its splendid colour. Under Capt. Parker's guidance I

51 The Land's End ... rocks 'fantastically shaped'.

went down a narrow winding passage in the rocks on the North side of the Land's End, and kneeling up on a flat piece of rock like a table which hangs over a horrible chasm, by craning over the abyss I could look through the great cavern which perforates the cliff behind the Land's End, and see the sea rushing through the cavern from the North to the South coast. It is said that a boat can sometimes pass through.

Probably the bridge which spans the cavern will give way some day, and the present Land's End will be an island. No doubt the Dollar Rock, the Armed Knight and

52 The Armed Knight.

other island rocks have been thus detached. Coming back we met a noisy rabble of tourists, males and females, rushing down the rocks towards the Land's End as if they meant to break their necks – and no great loss either. The rest of the insufferable snobs had of course been endeavouring to insult the ladies, and Capt. Parker suggested that a kicking might tend to mend their manners.

The Inn is built on the ridge of the bare down just above the Land's End. As we drove back through Sennen Church Town, in which parish the Land's End stands, we passed another Inn, with "The First House" written on the seaward side of the sign board, and "The Last House" on the reverse or landward side. Near Sennen Church Town stands the first mile stone, inscribed with I. as if it were the original mile of England.

Drive back to Penzance. On the road a boy threw a fir cone which struck a hamper and bounding hit the driver in the eye. At the Four Avenues we entered Penzance by another road. The driver said that once when he was driving an omnibus and four in hand from the Land's End to Penzance, on a very

53 Penzance – 'an old world picturesque place'.

dark night, directly he reached the crossroads of the Four Avenues he felt that something was wrong, and found that his leaders wanted to enter Penzance by one road, while his wheelers were going in by another. This manoeuvre had brought the leaders round to the omnibus door.

I like Penzance. It is an old world picturesque place.

We drove down the old long Market Jew Street, stopped at the fishmongers, and then past the Market Jew Chapel under repair where several coffined children have lately been found stuffed into holes and corners in the roof. Probably they were unbaptized children.

The Penzance people and especially the women are said to be the handsomest in Cornwall.

Back from Penzance by train. The tide was high and the Mount in a glorious flood of sunshine.

54 Market Jew Street, Penzance. (Detail from a view.)

Thursday, 28 July

Dora's birthday. Mrs H. drove H. and me to Truro in the pony carriage. Shopping, and then we joined the Truro Hockins and a party of their friends, young people chiefly, for a picnic down the river. We rowed or rather were rowed by boatmen down to Tregothnan, two boat loads of us, the hostess very nervous and fearful lest both boats should go to the bottom. We landed just above Tregothnan and walked up through pretty woods to the beautiful Church of St Michael Pen Kevil, restored by Lord Falmouth at a great expense.

The approach to the Church, which stands well on high ground, is along a broad sweeping drive through the woods and through a fine old granite pillar and ball gateway. A cruciform church like many of the Cornish churches, a beautiful pulpit, good stained glass and tiling, everything rich, handsome and in perfect taste.

Some of the party waited outside for us in the drive and we walked up to the house, and down the other hill to the boat house, just above which we had tea all across the road completely obstructing the thoroughfare. Our hostess reclined gracefully on her side up the slope of a steep bank, and thus enthroned or embedded dispensed tea and *heavy* cake and was most hospitable. The young ladies remarked with severity upon H. and myself for not being sufficiently attentive

55 The Church of St Michael Pen Kevil.

to their pretty wants. How could we be so inattentive to such fascinating creatures? They suggested it was because we were taking such uncommonly good care of ourselves. Listen to the voice of the Charmers. Is not this a caution to snakes? Charmeth she wisely?

I unhappily mistook butter for cream (Tell it not in Truro), and was much concerned about our hostess lest she should roll down the bank into the river. Also I was exceedingly puzzled to find out how it was that she did not so roll, for *what was to hinder it?*

The youngest girl, Agatha, I think, planted herself before me and demanded impetuously and imperiously in a loud voice, "What do *you* want?" "A kiss", said I mischievously, whereat she flung off in high disdain without a word. But being of a forgiving nature she presently returned and brought me some food.

After tea the young ladies rowed us across the river to see Old Kea Tower. The tide was too low to admit of our landing, but the pinnacles of the old tower looked pretty among the trees in the sunset.

Young lady affectations, peculiarities, vagaries &c &c – unintelligible. The evening scene was exceedingly beautiful, the glassy water, the falling tide, the woods sloping dark green to the water's edge, the anchored ships, "the stately ships going on to their haven under the hill" at Malpas, the old tower in the trees and the pinnacles clear against the sunset.

H. and our hostess had gone up to Tregothnan Gardens, but presently met us at the quay, and we all re-embarked and rowed home, a gentleman in each boat taking an oar to help the boatmen. Singing in each boat, and curlews calling and whistling from the banks. Low water and we could not get up to Truro, but were obliged to land at Lower Newham and scramble up the quay wall. Walk to Strangways Terrace a mile, supper, and drive home to Tullimaar late with lighted lamps.

Friday, 29 July

A most delightful expedition and picnic at Gurnard's Head. We drove to Camborne in the pony carriage and got to Rosewarne at 11. A large omnibus and pair was waiting to drive us on with the Parkers' party. I preferred going outside to see the country. Drove through Copper House, Phillack Church crowning the hill and Rivière, the bright white sand towans, and Lelant Church among the towans, the Church in the sand. Further on a glorious view back over beautiful blue St Ives Bay, the white lighthouse of Godrevy on the black island among the white foam of the breakers, and the brilliant sand hills of Phillack. The country red with corn, and a field of wheat reaped. The fish wives of St Ives bawling bass, fresh pilchard &c along the road. Past Knill's Monument above St Ives, leaving the town on the right on the other side of the hill. Then we came to a mine called St Ives Consols, and the works, rattling, clanking, clumping, at "stamping" and "streaming" tin. Asked the way here. The way not generally known, but the general impression was that we had come the wrong side of Rosewall Hill. Hard by was Towednack Church, and Towednack Hill, a notorious country for giants in old time (See Bot-

56 A fish wife.

57 St Ives Consols.

trell). The road not very bad, but the hills severe and our miserable horses nearly gruelled, almost fainting from thirst and fatigue, all abroad, scrambling and staggering all over the place. Once in a narrow part of the road the wheel tottered on the edge of a bank. We yawed about frightfully, the horses were too much done to pull straight or steady. Another lurch and we should all have gone head over heels into the field below, such a roly poly, broken bones if nothing worse and the doctor to pay. Happily there was one on board. Then the tire of the near fore wheel almost came off, and had to be inadequately tinkered on again. Captain Parker came outside with me. We were consulting his map and looking at the country. A sudden shout from the bowels of the omnibus, "Wo-way-halt, hold hard." – "What's the row" called Capt. Parker from the top of the omnibus, craning down to see what was the matter inside. "The sherry's flying all about" was the reply. "Miss Lewis has upset every drop of hers." – A roar of inextinguishable laughter. Sherry all round and "Proceed Edward". So we dragged on looking and longing for Zennor Church Town, and meeting people going to St Ives, seven wives and all.

Then we got a glimpse of the dim blue sea and the Gurnard's Head, far below us, stretching its head and neck out like a turtle crawling into the sea. The horses were driven into a pond in order to drink and cool their heels and tighten the tires of the omnibus wheels. (What a beautifully accidental couplet). Then we came to Zennor, the strange old town in the granite wilderness in a hollow of the wild hillside, a corner and end of the world, desolate, solitary, bare,

58 Gurnard's Head.

59 Zennor.

dreary, the cluster of white and grey houses round the massive old granite Church tower, a sort of place that might have been quite lately discovered, and where "fragments of forgotten peoples might dwell".

"None of your larks" said Capt. Parker occasionally and reprovingly to the people inside. But he was the most larky of the party. We were encouraged to hold on tight to the roof of the omnibus by the intelligence that a Captain — had fallen from the box seat of this very omnibus a few weeks ago and had been killed.

At last we got to the Gurnard's Head Hotel, the gentlemen walking across some fields while the ladies drove swiftly round.

Then the scrimmage of unpacking the hampers and everybody of course in everybody else's way. A capital dinner indoors, the Tullimaar *"dukes"* delicious and I actually ate and liked a slice of melon and, like Oliver Twist, asked for "more". "Oliver's asking for more". Memorable day. How do all the ghosts of those rejected melons now rise up and accuse me.

Dinner over and another scrimmage of repacking got through, we all streamed out down to the Head. We passed above a little cove approached by a slight scaffolding bridge, and Mrs H. wanted to go down to look for sea anemones, but the tide was too

60 Gurnard's Head Hotel.

high. Fishing boats lay up in this cove, sheltered from the stormy sea by a large guardian rock.

Oh that sunny happy evening gathering ferns among the cliffs, Asplenium Marinum, with its bright glossy green leaves, hiding itself so provokingly in the narrowest crevices of the rocks. I wandered round the cliffs to the broken rocks at the furthest point of the Head, and sat alone amongst the wilderness of broken shattered tumbled cliffs, listening to the booming and breaking of the waves below and watching the flying skirts of the showers of spray. Perfect solitude. The rest of the party were climbing about in the rocks somewhere overhead, but not a voice or sound was to be heard except the boom of the sea and the crying of the white-winged gulls. Not a sign or vestige of any other living thing.

A scramble up among the rocks to search for ferns for Mrs H. Not very successful, and H. had got her some much finer ones, but she did not despise mine, though they were very poor little ones in comparison.

The rest of the party had come down from a scrambling like goats and conies in the high rocks, the ladies having had to mount by means of the gentlemen's backs and knees.

We wandered slowly back through the corn fields to the inn, and never knew till afterwards that we had passed by the remains of a small ancient chapel which stands upon the neck or isthmus.

The last thing we saw of Gurnard's Head was a black line of cormorants sitting on the white salt-encrusted rocks.

A blacksmith had mended and riveted on the broken tire of our wheel, and while the horses were being put to after tea I went up to a row of children who were sitting on a wall like a line of sea-

61 Asplenium Marinum.

gulls, and talked to them about their school 2 miles off &c. They seemed nice children and reminded me of some of my Clyro pets, and two of the girls were very pretty with beautiful large dark eyes. They smiled and seemed inclined to be sociable, not at all shy, or awkward.

62 *Rosewarne House.*

We returned by Penzance, hearing it was a better road, and we did not repent of it. Soon after leaving the inn, we got a sight of the sea on both North and South coasts and the Mount in mist and twilight. A wooded fruitful valley soon took us down through market gardens to Penzance. It was getting very chilly on the top of the omnibus. (I wonder how Caesar liked travelling on the top of the diligence (summa diligentia) when he crossed the Alps). Mrs H. very kindly sent me out her waterproof cloak to put on and oh, how warm and comfortable it was. We left Penzance lighthouse behind, and then for a few minutes before we got to Hayle we caught the brilliant flash of the revolving light of Godrevy. We reached Camborne soon after 11 and sat down to dinner or supper at midnight, at Rosewarne that hospitable house, after depositing some of the party at their own houses in the town. Mrs Parker is an admirable hostess. I took her in to supper and had some talk with her about Wales and Monmouthshire where she used to live. She tells me, her brother has lately taken Bronllys Castle in Breconshire.

The dining room at Rosewarne is beautifully hung round with horns, antelope, stag, gnu, buffalo &c &c.

We left the hospitable house at 1 and got home about 3 in the morning. Daylight had not appeared, but it was a clear case of "we won't go home till morning". As we passed down the creek side the masts of a vessel showed against the sky. A sailing lighter had come up the creek at high tide with a load of limestone, and was lying at the quay waiting to unload and go down again with the next tide.

This morning we met two girls smartly dressed and driving cows to market with parasols up.

Saturday, 30 July

This morning helping H. to measure the walls of the ruinous old kennels, the material of which he proposes to sell to a builder.

There was a crafty rabbit formerly which used to devastate the place. All attempts to shoot, hunt or catch him were unavailing. He always disappeared suddenly in the kennels and no one could tell how he was lost or where he went to. At last it was discovered that, when closely pursued, he rushed into the kennels and bolted up the chimney of the boiling house, so out on to the top of a wall, jump on to a bank, and then out into the fields, over the hills and far away.

Today was the highest tide and the creek looked very pretty, filled with a broad flowing sheet of water covering all the sand banks and mud flats and reaching from shore to shore, the woods of Carclew glassed green in the quiet tide and the trees sweeping down their branches almost into the salt water.

In the evening, after dinner, H. took Juno the black retriever down to the creek for a swim. The dog plunged into the water delightedly after a stick and swam nearly across the creek, thoroughly enjoying her bathe. Flo sat afar off by the lodge gate, being afraid to come near lest she should be thrown in, and probably wondering at Juno's – to her – unintelligible love of plunging into water.

The tide was then ebbing and a boatload of people came rowing up the creek in the twilight against the tide. Then we went to help the gardener Richard Tresidder take a wasps' nest with slow powder. The nest lay very deep under the roots of a tree, and it was very difficult to find its whereabouts, and to dig it out.

Sunday, 31 July

Addie Cholmeley's birthday. We went to Church at 11 and 6.30 and in the afternoon sat under the ilex oak reading and talking.

In the evening we saw the new moon for the first time and I wished to go to Tintagel.
We wandered up and down the shady walk and the tide was high in the creek below. Then we strolled down the drive to the Truro Lodge and crossed the road deep in dust to a potato garden on the other side by the creek shore. The road was lively with people in groups, *"twoses* and *threeses".* The bright flower beds by the Lodge.

We explored the orchards and garden in search of fruit, ate some apples, and the filberts were nearly full.

Monday, Lammas Day

The morning opened with a dense sea fog, which turned to great heat during the day, close, oppressive and sultry. Reading Bottrell. Looking at Mrs H.'s beautiful copy of the Idylls of the King, Vivien, Elaine and Guinevere, illustrated by Doré. In the afternoon we were sitting on the garden seat under the copper beech, looking through the photograph albums. A storm seemed to be brewing, but it passed off after some mutterings of thunder and at 6 o'clock Mrs H. drove the pony carriage to Truro and took me with her. It was a very charming drive. We put up the carriage at the inn and Mrs H. went about her shopping, while I strolled about the town and leaned upon the bridge, watching the shipping and the boats with pleasure parties passing up and down the river under the bridge.

Tryst at the pastrycook's.

Coming home it was cool and pleasant. Shakespeare talk, Othello, Merchant of Venice, "the quality of mercy".

The owl and the baker's daughter. "They say the owl was a baker's daughter – We know what we are, but know not what we may be".

The escape from drowning, in New Zealand.

Polonius to Laertes.

> "The friends thou hast, and their adoption tried,
> Grapple them to thy soul with hooks of steel."

Today, or rather, last night it was settled that we set out for Tintagel on Tuesday. Three cheers.

> "Here's to the devil
> With his spade and wooden shovel
> Digging tin by the bushel
> With his tail cocked up."

> Verse of Miner's Song

With variations, e.g.

> "Did you ever see the devil

With his spade and wooden shovel
Digging 'tates' by the bushel
With his nightcap on?"

amendment on second reading suggested by Mrs Hockin.

Tuesday, 2 August

Another sea fog. As I sat writing in my bedroom before breakfast I heard the sound of voices talking and the rattle of oars in the rowlocks, and a boat came rowing up the creek on the high tide, almost, as it seemed, under the bedroom window, and after a few minutes dropped down the stream again.

At 4 p.m. we drove to Perranwell and took the train for Lostwithiel. About St Austell some of the streams were milk white with the China clay washings, and at Par a quantity of the white China clay was piled about the station waiting to be dispatched to the manufactories, as raw material. The evening was dull, heavy, sultry, and threatened rain. We walked from the station through the old-fashioned town carrying haversacks, bags &c &c past the fine Church with its beautiful spire to the Royal Talbot, a fine old coaching inn where they have stabling for 150 or 200 horses.

Supper ordered we sallied out again to walk to Restormel, about a mile out of the town. The country about Lostwithiel is exceedingly pretty, beautiful woods and bold hills all round, and the timber unusually fine, particularly the sycamores. The road to Restormel is kept like an approach to a gentleman's mansion, clipped hedges &c. Below bright green meadows watered and kept fresh by a little river, and above thick woods. The whole country looked green and fresh as if it had been rained on lately.

We crossed a tramway running into a low tunnel in a recess of the hillside. This tunnel is the adit of an iron mine which has been driven into the hillside. As we passed

63 Restormel Castle.

the mouth of the tunnel even at a little distance a rush of cold damp refreshing air struck us, and as we entered the tunnel the damp cold was icy. The banks all round the tunnel mouth were dripping with cool moisture, and ferns and other plants grew in luxuriant profusion. In directing us to Restormel Castle the landlady had told us we might if we liked go up to it through the wood. Seeing a path leading through the trees up the hill and a gate standing invitingly open we tried it, and soon found after a sharp pull up a steep hill that we had lost our way, and must come down again. At length condescending to ask our way, we were directed to go by a farmyard, and soon after we saw through the fine trees the low, massive, ivy-grown, heavily battlemented wall of the Castle. At the top of the hill a broad green ride between young fir plantations forms an avenue up a gentle rise to the Castle gate.

The place was new to us all. We were particularly struck by the perfect condition of the circular outer wall, which has scarcely a single stone out of place or the slightest appearance of ruin.

The Castle is one of the most remarkable I ever saw, small, circular, built on a steep green mound within a deep and perfect moat, crossed at the entrance to the Castle gate not by a drawbridge but by a bridge of ancient masonry over a culvert. The walls are very low, enormously thick, crowned with immensely large heavy ivy-covered battlements, and pierced thickly everywhere high and low with *holes* which we, after puzzling a long time over them, supposed to be arrow slits. The inner walls are pierced with these square holes, as thickly as the outer walls. These *holes* "exercised" us all and H. especially very much, and we kept on reverting to them thus, "But those *holes*, after all those *holes*. What is the meaning of those *holes*? What can they be for" &c &c. On the other side of the Castle from the entrance, in the place corresponding to the gateway, the Castle wall is supported and strengthened by a huge massive buttress rising from the bottom of the moat. The Castle stands on the top of a high slope in a small wood, with beautiful views of the woods and hills of the surrounding country, peeps and glimpses through the trees. Within, the Castle is no less extraordinary than without. There is an inner circular wall exactly answering to the outer one. In the space between these two walls are the Castle apartments, and all the centre of the Castle within the inner wall is an open circular court now grass grown, with doors opening into it all round from the several apartments. This round courtyard was probably always open to the sky, the only roofing having been between the two walls over the intervening space. A fine walk still exists along the top of the outer wall, just inside the great battlements, and we walked nearly all round the Castle, descending again where the walk was broken off, by an almost perfect flight of stone steps. We rambled and clambered about the ruined chambers up and down steps and breaches, puzzling over the meaning of what we saw, especially those inscrutable *holes*, wondering, guessing, speculating upon the use of the various rooms. We thought we could make out the kitchen, the guard room, the dungeon, the banqueting hall, and we assigned one room as the Chapel on the strength of an Ecclesiastically carved niche or canopy like that of a credence table or piscina. The Castle walls were so low that the turf of the mound without came nearly up on to a level with the sill of the banqueting hall window. We found a deep recess in the wall with a deep pit below it which struck me as looking like a dog kennel, and which we afterwards thought must have been used as a wild beasts' den, as we heard that there is a tradition that the old Kings of Cornwall once lived in this Castle and kept wild beasts for hunting and fighting. And indeed the Castle is a strange weird place and looks as if it belonged to an older world. So little is known of it, no one to show it, or explain it, or speak to about it, or to ask a question of. "Ah" said one of our party, "if these walls could but speak and tell their own tale". But the Castle stands by itself, so lone, so silent in its woods, and so perfect at first sight in the approach up the avenue, that it gives one a feeling of awe, and expectation, a feeling almost of fear, as if the old giant or king who lived there had gone out into the woods or country round to hunt or fight, and had not thought it worth while to shut his castle gate but had left it wide open and might return at any moment. It seemed to me a very awful place.

It gave me the idea that it was not quite deserted, and that we might find someone yet in the chambers round the court.

Happily we were uninterrupted and the spell was unbroken, and the charm remains and now will remain.

The still, close, rather sombre evening exquisitely suited the place, and the time and place left a strange impression on my mind.

Wednesday, 3 August

Breakfast at 7 and a waggonette and pair ordered at 7.30, but of course it did not come round till 8.15, when we started with a game bay horse and a slug of a chestnut mare to drive to Tintagel by Camelford.

Climbing some steep pitches out of Lostwithiel towards Bodmin we saw to advantage the lovely broken scenery round Lostwithiel. Round blue hills and rich corn and meadow valleys, and the hillsides clothed with thick woods. The combes and deep narrow lanes reminded one of Devonshire. We passed Lanhydrock, Lord Robarts' fine place, and extensive woods on the left, and left Bodmin on the left down in the hollow, a poor-looking town.

On the hill above and beyond Bodmin a lofty monument stood up against the sky, a column erected in memory of Colonel Gilbert.

For some distance beyond Bodmin the roads were straight and level. Then they became hilly, and the hills were sometimes very steep. In this broken hilly country there had been rain lately, the roads were soft and damp, the hedges and banks full of lovely ferns were dripping and sparkling, and everything looked fresh, moist, and tender bright green. Our driver did not know the way, we had to ask the road continually and once or twice we nearly went wrong. We crossed some beautiful brooks or small rivers looking like trout streams, and in the midst of one grew an enormous Osmunda.

64 Lanhydrock.

As we neared Camelford the sky lowered gloomily, it grew very dark and a few drops fell. Then with scarcely any warning such a thundershower burst upon us as I have seldom been out in. Spoilt by the long indulgence of fine weather, we had only Mrs H.'s small umbrella amongst us three, and nothing beside except our walking sticks, not a mackintosh, overcoat or anything, nothing but our walking sticks, and Mrs H. had not even a waterproof. The furious rain lashed, drove and streamed into the carriage till we feared Mrs

65 *Camelford.*

H. would be wet through. At last she conceived the brilliant idea of sitting down on the floor of the waggonette while we sat on each side to shield her from the tremendous rain which seemed to grow more fearful every moment, I holding the little umbrella over her head while H. wrapped a rug lent by the driver round her, holding it up tight round her throat till she looked, as someone said, as if she were in a barber's shop going to be shaved. However it kept her pretty dry. Keeping quite dry in such rain and with such appliances was out of the question.

So we sat and drove hard and the rain drove harder, and we longed for Camelford. But Camelford seemed a long way off.

At length we found ourselves dashing down the long steep narrow street of Camelford, to the amazement and amusement of the natives.

A rush and scramble into the inn shaking ourselves like water dogs, the carriage was driven rapidly off to the stables and Boots carried off our coats, the cushions &c to the kitchen fire. Ten minutes earlier and we should have avoided the storm for it soon broke, the sun came out and we drove on again.

The storm had been very partial, for a mile out of Camelford on the Tintagel road it had not rained a drop and the roads were dusty.

Now we got into a slate country. The fences were of slate and we passed by the Bowithick slate quarries, a wild strange country, the road passing between high cliffs and bastions of slate in piles, or stone banks supporting the sides of the slate quarries.

Then we got a glimpse of the sea from the top of a hill, a blue haze and as smooth as oil, and in this dreamy sea stood a large black rock. The white houses of Trevena lay before us on high ground, and dark long Tintagel Church crowned a cliff over-looking the sea.

We put up the horses at Trevena, at the Wharncliffe Arms, next door to the house where Mr G. Venables used to stay with Mr Cook of the Saturday Review. On the grass plat in front of the house stood a large white wooden figure of a sea gull, an old ship figure head. We had lunch and then started for Tintagel, taking with us a guide book to Cornwall which we had found in the inn room.

We were told to ask at the cottage in the valley for the Castle key and a guide. The said cottage was a little low house which was or had been a mill. It was built on the edge of a little stream beneath the cliffs, upon which we could see the Castle keep far above. The cottage was built in a sort of hole beneath the level of the ground or rather of the road. You went down steps to the front door and when within you went down steps again into the best room. The little garden in front was gay with nasturtiums and other flowers. An old man with a red face was hobbling round the garden with a stick. He called to his daughter for the key and in honour of the young lady volunteered to

66 Tintagel.

67 Doré's picture of the finding of Arthur by Merlin.

be our guide, a great favour and mark of respect, as the old man usually sends his daughter to show the Castle to visitors.

The first place we came to was a cove with boats drawn up in it and a large cave piercing the cliff through. They have just begun mining for iron in this cliff. The old man said that this cove was called "the King's Cove" or "King Arthur's Cove".

On the other side of the low narrow neck of land which joins the otherwise island cliff to the mainland is another cove, and it seems as if in course of time the intervening isthmus would be worn away and the so-called island become one in reality.

We had been reading and thinking a great deal lately about Guinevere, Arthur and Merlin, and we conjectured as to the place where Merlin found Arthur after the great storm, a naked child, "Upon the sands, of wild Dundagil by the Cornish sea". We wondered if it might have been one of these coves, and tried to discern a likeness between the rocks of these coves to the cliffs in Doré's fine picture of the finding of Arthur by Merlin.

The dream come true.

The two cliffs on each of which a part of the Castle stands, and which were once joined at the top by a drawbridge, are now divided by an enormous chasm, which slopes and narrows down gradually to the little isthmus which joins them together at the base. Crossing this little neck of land from cove to cove, we commenced ascending the island cliff by a good but narrow zig zag path lately cut in the face of the cliff. Presently we were stopped by a wall heavily battlemented. The old man produced a key and unlocked a door in the wall, and admitted us into the precincts of the Castle spreading over the summit of the cliff. We were much surprised by the extent of the Castle. I had expected to see two or three tall towers beetling on the cliff edge. But the remains of buildings and fortifications spread over a large part of the island.

Like Restormel, the Castle of Tintagel is Duchy property and is not let fall utterly to pieces. Sheep are brought up the cliff and allowed to graze amongst the ruins.

The work of the Castle is so ancient, simple and primitive, that it looks almost like the natural rock in parts, and as there is so much rock scattered about or cropping up alive through the turf in masses and walls, it is difficult to tell at a little distance which is rock and which fabulously ancient, time-worn, rude weather-beaten masonry, or where the rock ends and the masonry begins.

This Castle is pierced full of square *holes*, in the inner as well as the outer walls, like Restormel. The "saddle bits" are very perfect.

Some of the walls have a curve as if they were fragments of round towers or circular walls.

The Chapel walls remain, three feet high, with traces of doors and window, the stone seats along either side of the porch, and the rude under-masonry which supported the altar. A broad slab, rather oblong, lay near the altar and may have been the slab which covered the altar, or a tombstone.

The Chapel must have been quite a small one.

The only bit of carving we saw was on the edge of a stone lying by the altar beautifully carved with the quatre foil.

Some distance further on is the graveyard, with some of the small footstones still standing erect at the foot of the graves. It is a very solemn place this graveyard on the cliff, the ancient strange forgotten people, so long, so quietly asleep in their storm-swept graves.

Still further on is a hollow in the uneven surface of the cliff, a low curious hole in the side of the slope, which is called the Hermit's Cave, but which is much more like the mouth of an underground passage leading down to [a] little well in the lower ground in a sheltered part of the island.

There is a grim significance in the absence of fortifications on the north-western side of the island, and when one stands upon the edge of the cliffs and looks down, one sees the reason why it was not thought needful to fortify this side.

On the highest point I picked up the grey feather of a gull and brought it away as a remembrance.

Our guide pointed out the Pinnacle Rock, a slender square pillar rising from the foot of the cliffs but standing away from them a little.

He also showed us King Arthur's Chair, a large flat rock in which several round holes are scooped, which look as if they had been used in playing some rude game like "Nine Holes". A ledge of rock below the seat serves for a footstool, and the chair is canopied by an enormous slanting piece of rock which stretches and projects overhead and meets the back of the Chair seat at an acute angle.

We were shown the recess or shelf in the cliff where the drawbridge used to rest.
It is said that the chasm was cut wider at first purposely, to ensure the greater safety of the island part of the Castle. Time, wave and weather have probably done the rest.

From above the sea appeared as smooth as oil, but in the caves beneath, the waves were breaking with a grand boom like thunder deep and low, which seemed to shake the whole island.

A white ghostly "mist clung like a face cloth to the face" of the sea. The Gull Rock, island, loomed dimly through the white haze of the tremendous heat, not a fierce heat, for the sun was almost veiled, but a damp close still heat, most sultry, oppressive and trying to bear. There was scarcely any view. Northwards the mist cleared a little and the sea looked blue, but elsewhere it was a dead sickly white, and Trevose Head was nowhere to be seen.

The walls of the keep and Castle buildings on the mainland are more thick and massive than those on the island, being more exposed to assault and battery. The real strength and defence of the island Castle is its position. We did not mount the cliff to examine the mainland part of the Castle. From the island we saw Tintagel Church on the opposite hill, and in the churchyard the tombstone of Mr Cook. His boat in the cove seems now to be the property of Mr Kinsman, the clergyman of Tintagel, for it bears both names.

We bought some photographs of Tintagel Castle at the mill as we returned, and then loitered back to the inn through the dreadful heat and had dinner.

We left Trevena a little before four and enjoyed the cool pleasant drive back to Lost-withiel, which we reached about 7.30. Indeed before we got in, the air had turned rather chilly. Cornish evenings are apt to be chilly even in the hottest weather.

We reached the station just in time for the train and returned to Truro by the "Flying Dutchman", but alas, as Mrs H. said quaintly, "he flieth not below Plymouth", and we were a long time getting to our journey's end, all of us I think going to sleep on the way. I know I did.

Thursday, 4 August

A quiet day, and I am sure Mrs H. must have needed one. In the afternoon I walked about the grounds taking a farewell of all my favourite places, and paid a visit to the greenhouse and passion flower, and the white heather bush in the Truro Lodge drive. Went down to the Falmouth Lodge and along the road to the Truro Lodge under the beautiful bank purple with heath, and pausing by the creek shore where the tide was low, to look up and down the beautiful valley, seen at its best in the soft golden after-noon sunshine, the white cluster of houses at Devoran down the reach of yellow sand, and above, the grey mansion of Goon Vrea in its woods, the blue hills, tall foundry chimneys and white cottages by the creek shore beneath the woods and hills seen through the soft haze of curling smoke.

Music and singing in the drawing room after dinner.

> Robin Adair
> Ye banks and braes of bonnie Doon
> Annie Laurie
> Maggie's Secret
> Susan's [Story]

The Carnival of Venice

> "Come to me when daylight sets,
> Sweet, then come to me – "

Sad music,

> Auld Robin Gray,
> "I darena think on Jamie, for that
>   would be a sin –
>
>   —
>

And auld Robin Gray is a good man to me"

>   —
>
> "No more she could weep, her tears were a' spent
> *Despair* it was come and she thought it *content*
> She thought it content, but her cheek it grew pale
> And she drooped like a lily broke down by the hail."

Children's voices.

Friday, 5 August

The last pleasant excursion. The last happy day. Martin had been sent to Falmouth overnight for a carriage and horse, and brought back a grey heavy horse and hooded carriage in which he drove us this morning to Godrevy.

We called at Camborne (Rosewarne) to leave an Inverness cloak which Capt. Parker lent me to drive home in last Friday, and the kind hospitable people made us promise to call on our return and have supper or something.

Redruth market and people hurrying about with conger eels.

Sorrowful dreams.

We met with several sharp white squalls and had all to crowd for shelter under the hood with an umbrella up in front. H. suggested that passers by would say, "There go a lady and gentleman with a child". The road led us along the top of the cliffs. The carriage was stopped by a gate and we got out to look down "Hell's Mouth". Standing on the turf edge of the cliff you look down sheer into a small narrow semi-circular cavern, into which the sea roars and boils at a horrible depth below.

Leaving Mrs H. in the carriage to drive on to Gwythian Church Town, H. and I struck across the down to see the British Church buried in the sand.

We came to the place suddenly and without warning, and looked down

68 The church buried in the sand.

into the Church as into a long pit. The sand is drifted solid up to the very top of the outside walls. The walls are about four feet high measured from the inside. So far they are almost perfect. The material is granite with a good deal of pure felspar, of which I brought away a pretty pink piece. The Church is quite a small building, oblong, a door and window place still perceptible, and the faint remains of the rude pillars of a chancel arch still to be made out. Within the memory of persons still living the altar was still standing, but the place has got into the hands of a dissenting farmer who keeps the place for a cattle yard and sheep fold

69 Gwithian church and school.

and what more need be said. I do wish that some people of influence in the neighbourhood would bestir themselves and rescue from utter destruction and oblivion this most interesting relic of the earliest British Christianity, that which came to us direct from the East.

Probably there was a Christian Church at Gwythian before St Augustine landed in England to bring us the Roman version of Christianity.

These sand hills are very restless, always shifting. They overwhelm ancient buildings and then reveal them after they have been hidden for centuries. The sand passes on in its progress to form hills elsewhere and gives up its prey. Suddenly the monument and relic of an older world and more primitive ancient simple religion is revealed.

The sand and the centuries have been kinder than the dissenting farmer.

70 Godrevy Lighthouse.

We found Mrs H. waiting for us at Gwythian Church Town. Crossing the moor we caught sight of the top of Godrevy Lighthouse over the line of sand towans, and heard the roaring of the sea.

I took a great fancy to this village by the sea, with its nice Church and schools. We went to the Curate's (Mr Urquhart) picturesque little cottage lodgings, but he was not at home and we met him coming out of the lychgate from working in his churchyard among some new walks and flower beds he is making. He showed us over the "severely correct" cruciform Church with the usual Cornish tower, and walked with us round the churchyard, which he is making very pretty, discussing his plans and alterations. Some of the carved stone work of the old Church is built into the lychgate, and some other fragments lie about upon the walls. The Curate complained a good deal about the people and their ineradicable tendency to dissent.

In the churchyard is the grave of a former Curate of Gwythian, a Mr Drury, who was drowned amongst the rocks near Godrevy on Palm Sunday evening, 1865.

It is supposed that his dog pulled him into one of those horrible deep chasms and crevices amongst the rocks, or that he fell in whilst playing with his dog and pushing him into the water, for he was a beautiful swimmer and would not have been drowned probably in open water. The body was found among the rocks by a man gathering sand or seaweed on the shore, and brought home in his cart.

There is a coloured window in the Church to Drury's memory.

In the churchyard, overhanging the road is a magnificent fruit-bearing fig tree, covering a vast space of ground. The figs on the top of the tree only, ripen and become fit to eat.

The horse was put in the carriage again and we drove heavily through the deep sand to the shore, passing a Red River and tin stamping works rattling clanking pounding away amongst the sand hills.

The horse was put up at a farm house and Martin ordered to beg, borrow or (– not steal, but) take some corn for him, and then bring up the luncheon hamper to the rocks.

Meanwhile we walked along the cliffs and passed a second "Hell's Mouth" much more fearful than the first, deeper, narrower, and the sea rushing into the chasm with terrible violence.

We meant to have gone across in a boat to Godrevy to see the lighthouse, but the sea was too rough for a boat to put out or to land at the rocks, over which the spray was shooting and flying in white clouds. There was a heavy groundswell going, the legacy probably of some storm in the Atlantic. The sea was all in a roar and tumult, dark grey and stained brown and muddy by the stirring up of the sand, the waves, rolling in heavily over the rocks, leaping and dashing against the cliffs. Round the rocks of the island the sea was all in a work of white foam and wild breakers, the whole bay heaving wild and dark, and the waves fretting white over the treacherous points of black rock around the bell buoy.

It was rather provoking that the day we wanted to cross to the lighthouse should be the only rough day I have seen. *"And yet"* 'tis an ill wind that blows no one any good, and it was a grand sight to watch the sea in his power.

Martin appeared with the rug and basket, and we had luncheon, *Queen, Church and State*, in the shadow of a rock, in a nook of the cliffs overlooking the sea.

Martin amused me by retiring to a respectful distance with his share of the provender and grinning over a rock, nothing but his black head to be seen, like a seal with a tall hat on.

After luncheon we went down on the beach to look for sea anemones among the rocks and pools at low water for Mrs H. We found a few red specimens, and she found a green one.

H. and I went out nearly to the end of the rocks where the waves were plunging and flying in foam over the reef, and presently we saw a large seal a hundred yards off fishing among the rocks near the shore. His black head was like a dog swimming and something like the head of a man. He dived suddenly, then came up again, disappeared again, and once more appeared with his large black shiny head not more than 50 yards from us, stationary, floating and riding easily, rising and falling with the swell, sometimes looking round at us with his great bright eye. It was the first seal I had ever seen wild, and I was delighted.

"The last sigh of the moon."
The last longing lingering farewell look at the Cornish sea.

The white sand towans of Phillack, Lelant Church among the sand, St Ives and the great bay, the crest of St Michael's Mount, the Portreath lighthouse and Trevose Head, so exquisitely clear was the air.

Grapes and claret on a grassy bank, and we drove back to Camborne, reaching Rosewarne at 7.

We walked round the pretty flower gardens and fine kitchen garden and visited the ferns and fruit houses. Dinner at 8, and a most admirable conger eel. I had no idea conger was so good, or good at all.

The "infant" Clare, and the two beautiful white cats.

As we drove away the Church clock struck ten, and the granite pillars sparkled in the moonlight.

Home at midnight and hot supper, roast fowl &c.

Packing till after one.

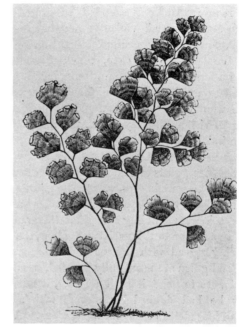

71 Maidenhair fern.

Saturday, 6 August

Up at 6. Finished packing and rushed down the Truro drive to get some sprays from the bush of white heather.

The trees were all dripping from early showers, the tears of the morning. The morning was fresh, cool and lovely, and the beautiful place looked more beautiful than ever.

H. drove me and my luggage to the first train, 7.35. A hurried rush but we arrived a minute too late. There was nothing for it but to leave the luggage at the Station and return to Tullimaar, to wait for the next train at 11.5. After the first feeling of annoyance and disappointment I was glad to have missed the train, as it gave me another pleasant morning.

We finished breakfast comfortably and then H. took me down to see the Holy Well in a little garden croft by the Falmouth Lodge. It is a dropping well and the clear cold water drips over, from the arched roof of a little cave cut in the rock side, into a small basin scooped in the living rock. The little cave is dark and cool, overhung with briers from the bank above, and ferns grow about it, and dip their fronds almost into the water. The brimming basin overflows softly and drippingly into the grass, and the rocky brim is worn smooth by the resting of buckets when people come to the well to draw. It is a very beautiful well and reminds one of a holy water niche and basin. It is called St Katharine's Well, or the Holy Well. The water is celebrated for its sweetness, coldness and purity, to which I can bear witness having drunk three draughts of it.

Martin says, if he had this well in London, he might leave off work and sell water.

The morning sunshine and shadows of the overhanging trees chequered and dappled the fishpond, and the gold and silver fish gleamed as they sailed from shadow into sunlight.

72 'Sprays of white heather'.

73 Truro station.

Mrs H. was planting ferns, thc Gurnard's Head Asplenium, in the potting house, and I leaned on the window sill outside watching her and making her laugh with Cowper's "Tithing Time".

"The Parson merry is and blithe" &c.

The second parting.

And so endeth a very happy time.

The drooping of transplanted flowers and the withering of tendrils torn from their clasp.

Notes

Page 21. *Windmills whirling* these two words have been inserted into the text after the rest was written. Most of the windmills in Somerset were concentrated in this area, between the Rivers Axe and Parret, on ridges such as the Poldens and Sedgemoor Hill, and higher ground rising above the Levels. Almost all had ceased working by the end of the nineteenth century.

Page 22. *I had quite forgotten ...* Kilvert had probably never seen this station before. On his childhood visits to Devon he would have passed through the old St David's Station, built in Pennyroyal Fields in 1844. The new St David's, in Doric style with ironwork by Kerslake of Exeter, was completed in 1864.

Page 23. *the house where we lodged* Kilvert's parents had usually taken the family to the sea for summer holidays. His sister Emily also recalled the stay at Dawlish: 'Once we went to Dawlish for part of the holidays, going on to Teignmouth for the latter part ...' See 'The "Rambling Recollections" of Mrs E.J. Wyndowe' (Emily Kilvert) in *More Chapters from the Kilvert Saga* (Hereford: Kilvert Society, n.d.), p.109.

Page 23. *the Ivy Bridge viaduct* Brunel's viaducts on the South Devon and Cornwall railways were famous for their dramatic construction of timber beams on stone piers. The Ivy Bridge viaduct was the highest on this stretch of the South Devon Railway (114 feet max.); others nearly as high were Blachford (107 feet) and Slade (100 feet). The timber viaducts were particularly frequent in Cornwall: Kilvert would have crossed no fewer than thirty-four between Plymouth and Truro. Most were replaced by masonry viaducts by the end of the century; the last disappeared under an embankment in the 1930s.

Page 24. *The Cornish mail carriages* 'The only vehicle calling for notice [on the Cornwall Railway] was the solitary Mail Van, which worked on the Night Mails between Plymouth and Falmouth for many years, and later on to and from Penzance, known to the Post Office as the "Cornwall T.P.O.". This was distinguished from other Travelling Post Offices by having, instead of the usual Royal Arms, the Three Feathers and "Ich Dien" motto of the Duke of Cornwall emblazoned on its panels.' (E.T. MacDermot, *History of the Great Western Railway*, II, pp.295–6).

Page 24. *Tullimaar* William Hockin finally inherited Tullimaar as a result of a Chancery Court case. Benjamin Sampson, who built the house, had died in 1840, and his widow Ann had continued to live there until her death in

1852. The estate then passed to his nephew, Benjamin Sampson the younger (who had changed his name from Benjamin Sampson Cloak in 1840), with a reversion to the younger Benjamin's sister and her heirs. This sister was Ann Sampson Hockin, William Hockin's mother. She had married the Revd Henry William Hockin, Vicar of Stithians and Perranarworthal, in 1836, but had died in 1844, two years before her husband. When Benjamin Sampson the younger died unmarried in 1864 it was found that he had ignored the reversion clause in his uncle's will and left his considerable estates to business associates, William Shilson and others. The ensuing dispute was resolved by William Hockin acquiring Tullimaar and a settlement of £12,000, including £1,000 for each of his two sisters, while Shilson took the rest of the Sampson estate.

Tullimaar has had an interesting subsequent history. General Eisenhower stayed there briefly before D-Day in 1944, and reputedly suffered an assassination attempt by an American soldier. In 1957 the estate was bought by Princess Marthe Bibesco, a descendant of Napoleon and celebrated French literary hostess of the inter-war years, who lived there until her death in 1973.

Page 24. *the two years' dream* It was only around sixteen months since the Hockins had left Langley Lodge to live in Tullimaar, but two years since it had become certain that William would inherit the house. This sentence was added later in a different ink.

Page 25. *an iron foundry* The Perran Foundry at Perran Wharf, Perranarworthal, founded by the Fox family in 1791, and the first important ironworks in Cornwall. It covered an area of nearly six acres, and employed around 400 men. The foundry closed in 1879, after which the buildings were used for making animal foodstuffs and grinding corn.

Kilvert originally left a space after 'the white walls and chimneys of a', which he filled in later in different ink, presumably when he found out what the buildings were. Similarly, just above he first wrote 'up the river' and 'down the river' the wrong way round, scratching the words out and correcting them when he found which way the stream flows.

Page 25. *Eliza Killing* One of the Killing family of Langley Burrell: in the Census return of 1871 (for Tullimaar), her place of birth is given as Langley Burrell, and her age as 18. Four other members of the Killing family are mentioned elsewhere in the Diary.

Page 26. *... stand on an island* There is no evidence today of the houses standing 'on an island', and it is difficult to see how they ever could have done. Local people have no explanation for the reference, and large-scale late nineteenth-century plans of the area belonging to Mr Leslie Dale of Churchtown Farm (next door to Tullimaar) offer no clue either. The most that one could say is that Tullimaar and all the hill behind it are on a sort of peninsula between the River Kennal flowing through Perran Wharf, the Carnon River flowing into Restronguet Creek, and the Trewedna Stream that flows between Perranwell and Perranwell Station. Probably Kilvert had been misled by the Cornish extension of the word 'island', as with the Cornish equivalent 'enys', to mean a peninsula (cf. The Island at St Ives, or the manor and estate of Enys within two miles of Tullimaar, which occupies a similar position above the confluence of two streams that flow into Mylor Creek). The phrase 'the island home' was 'in the air' at this time: for example, there was a popular sentimental song

'Come to My Island Home' written by W.P. Newenham around 1840, with music by Wm. McGhie; an adventure story for boys published in Kilvert's youth, *The Island Home; or, the Young Cast-Aways* (1852) by 'Christopher Romaunt' (J.F. Bowman), set in the South Seas; and the latest stage success in London, advertised in *The Times* just as Kilvert started his holiday, was 'the new fantastical entertainment, *Our Island Home*', written by W.S. Gilbert with music by German Reed.

Page 26. *Lander the African traveller* Kilvert left a large space for the name, and put in 'Lander' later. Richard Lemon Lander (1804–34) discovered the source of the Niger. The Doric column, erected in 1835, was designed by the local deaf and dumb architect Philip Sambell, but fell down through defective workmanship a year later. The statue on the rebuilt column is by the Cornish sculptor Nevill Northey Burnard.

Page 26. *the ugly cupola Church* St John's in Lemon Street, built in 1827. The unusual design, often described as 'Italian', was also by Philip Sambell. It was considerably enlarged in 1860, and later further altered in 1884.

Page 27. *a nice clean town* The system of leats dating back to the eighteenth century was frequently admired by visitors, although the little streams themselves came to be seen as potentially serious sources of pollution. See H.L. Douch, *The Book of Truro* (Chesham, 1977), pp.111–15.

Page 27. *The fine old Church of St Mary* Demolished in 1880 to make way for the Cathedral. However, the richly ornamented south aisle, of seven bays – the part admired here by Kilvert – was preserved and incorporated into the Cathedral, on the south side of the chancel.

Page 28. *Danish and Norwegian ships* ... Although Truro was still officially a port at this date, the silting-up of the channel between Malpas and Truro meant that cargoes generally had to be taken on by barge from Malpas. Norwegian timber for the mines, one of Truro's main imports, had since the eighteenth century been towed in rafts from Malpas and stored in pounds along the river.

Page 29. *It has been compared to the Rhine* ... By Queen Victoria, on a steam-boat trip up the river in September 1846. Her remark ('This equals the Rhine') is reported in E.S. Tregoning's *History of Falmouth* of 1865 (p.110). Kilvert himself would have known the Rhine from the holiday he took in Switzerland, Germany and France in 1869.

Page 29. *King Harry's Passage* The boatman's unlikely story is told in Polwhele's *The Civil and Military History of Cornwall*, vol. IV (Exeter, 1806), p.35, n.: 'King Harry passage ... is said by tradition to be denominated from one of our royal Harries, who in some troubles of his reign retired into Cornwall, and swam the river on horseback, though about 400 or 500 yards broad: and some say he was Harry the 4th.' Henry VIII has also been proposed as a candidate. Charles Henderson, however, considered that the name comes from a chapel dedicated to King Henry VI in Chapel Wood above the passage (*Old Cornish Bridges and Streams* (Truro, 1928), p.90).

Page 30. *Oyster dredgers were at work* ... The only technical description in this notebook, and an exactly accurate account of the dredging of oysters ('haul and towing') in the Fal as it is still done today, the last fishery of its kind in the world. Several of the boats still used are nearly 100 years old. Kilvert's description is particularly interesting in that the dredgers were clearly not observing the season that is observed today (October–March, 9 a.m.–3 p.m.); it was overdredging that greatly reduced the fishery by the end of the century. (Information from Mr D.M. Laity, oyster-dredger, of Flushing.) In the line above, the word 'boatman' has been added beneath the line in pencil; the writer's eye must have slipped while copying up.

Page 30. *The guard ship Ganges ...* The last 'wooden wall' of the Navy had been moored at the then Naval dockyard at Mylor for training since 1866. *Ganges* was towed away for breaking up in 1899.

Page 30. *The Harbour has an unfinished look ...* The foundation stone of the Docks was laid in 1860, and they were never completed as intended.

Page 31. *The new Hotel* The Falmouth Hotel, built near the new railway station in 1865 (the railway was opened in 1863).

Page 31. *a wreck ... on the Stags' Horns* The ship was the *Scottish Queen*, of Sunderland, sailing from Odessa to Falmouth. Kilvert seems to have been misled by this into thinking that it was a Russian ship: some at least of the foreign-sounding crew were probably Wearsiders! The captain, who 'looked very foreign and Russian', was actually called Errington. Kilvert's report of the wreck differs in some details from accounts in the local papers: the *West Briton* (21 July) times the wreck at 6.45 a.m., the *Falmouth Packet and Cornwall Advertiser* (23 July) at 7 a.m. (calling the ship the 'Scotia's Queen', of 357 tons register), and the *Cornish Telegraph* (27 July) times it at 7.30 a.m., giving the ship's size as 450 tons register and the cargo as 'between 700 and 800 tons of wheat'.

Page 31. *Captain Adam* The stepson of the Revd R.L. Venables, Kilvert's vicar in Clyro. He is mentioned several other times in the Diary.

Page 32. *the Royal Cornwall Sailors' Home* Kilvert had left a line blank at this point, and these words have been inserted in pencil, in a different hand.

Page 32. *Friends in Council* The phrase is taken from the title of a discursive and improving work by Sir Arthur Helps, Clerk of the Privy Council, which went through several editions in the 1850s and 1860s: *Friends in Council: a series of readings and discourse thereon*, 2 vols (London, 1847; a second series followed in 1859). The words are used here as a convenient cliché, rather than intending any specific reference to the contents of the book.

Page 32. *the old ruined castle on Carn Brea* The old castle was not entirely a ruin: it had been restored and enlarged in the eighteenth and nineteenth centuries, and was let to tenants. Kilvert strangely never mentions what is by far the most dramatic feature of Carn Brea, the massive granite monument erected in 1836 to commemorate Francis Basset, Lord de Dunstanville (1757–1835). This stands 90 feet high on the central summit of Carn Brea, itself 828 feet above sea level, and dominates the countryside for miles around.

Page 32. *"Thou art Lord of the world, bright Tin"* Taken from William Bottrell, *Traditions and Hearthside Stories of West Cornwall* (Penzance, 1870; reprinted Newcastle upon Tyne, 1970), in the story of the Giants of Towednack, p.31: 'when the shades of evening fell on the hills, a bonfire was made on the Garrack zans (holy rock) before the door, around which they danced hand-in-hand whilst the tinkard harped and sang, "Thou art lord of the world, bright tin!'". Plomer misread the line as 'Thou art Lord of the world-bright tin!', in which puzzling form it has since been quoted as an old tinners' song. Among the subscribers to the first edition of Bottrell's work were Tennyson and Miss S. Hockin, H.'s aunt (see note to p.34 below). Curiously, Kilvert does not describe himself as reading the book until Monday 25 July.

Page 33. *"Bal" (mine) girls* ... Bal maidens worked on the surface, breaking rocks and dressing ore; their distinctive headgear gave protection from the sun. Large numbers were employed in all the Cornish mines until the early years of this century (*bal* is an old Cornish word for a mine).

Page 33. *La Rivière* The gentrification of an old name of uncertain origin, also spelt 'Revyer', and locally pronounced 'Rovier'. The estate of Rivierc had only recently been purchased from the defunct Cornish Copper Co. (in June 1870) by the Revd Frederick Hockin, Rector of Phillack with Gwithian from 1853 to 1902 and uncle of H.; he also owned the advowson of Phillack. He paid £4,600 for the estate, which covered 167 acres and included the Towans, Clifton Terrace, and Riviere Farm as well as Riviere House. Compton Mackenzie lived in the house forty years later, from 1908 to 1910, and he described the house and superbly-stocked gardens at length in his autobiography, *My Life and Times, Octave 4, 1907–1915* (London, 1965), pp.40–1.

Page 34. *Miss Hockin* Susan Hockin, aunt of H. The nieces were his two sisters, Anne Sampson Hockin (1837–1928) and Deborah Margaret Hockin (1839–1932). The

'fine-looking grandfather and grandmother' were the Revd William Hockin (1776–1853), Rector 1809–53, and Peggy, née Williams (1779–1866), of Madron. The Rectory and its gardens still largely conform to Kilvert's description, although he describes as a bow window what was and is a deep bay window. The old back kitchens have been taken down, and the stables were demolished when the road by the church was widened. The figurehead has long since gone from the garden.

Page 34. *a curate came in* ... The Revd William Horsburgh, Incumbent of St Elwyn, Hayle. The couple were Henry Pool, aged 44, an engine-fitter of Bodriggy, and Elizabeth Hambly Grose (née Stevens), a widow of 41 from Hayle. A note on the marriage certificate by the Revd Frederick Hockin declares it null and void, 'the above-named Elizabeth Hambly Grose being a sister of the deceased wife of the above-mentioned Henry Pool'.

Page 35. *the slaughter of the children of St Felicitas* ... Kilvert has imagined this. The window is not nearly so lurid, showing simply a static pose of St Felicitas with the children grouped in front of her. One child embraces a large red diagonal cross-shaped sword, whose golden handle is held by the Saint as she shelters the children in her cloak.

Page 35. *"towans"* An old Cornish word, still of course in common use, meaning sand-dunes (cf. Welsh *tywyn*, sea-shore, sand-dune). These towans were part of the property recently purchased by the Rector.

Page 36. *a St Ives man named Knill* ... John Knill (1737–1811), sometime Mayor of St Ives, Treasurer of Gray's Inn, and reputed pirate, built Knill Steeple on Worvas Hill as a mausoleum for himself in 1782. He endowed it so that, every five years, ten young girls under ten years of age and two widows aged over 64 should dance around the monument accompanied by a fiddler, and sing the Hundredth Psalm. The ceremony first took place in 1801, in his lifetime, and has been held every five years without interruption ever since.

Page 36. *"Who whipped the hake?"* One of the proverbial jokes, originating in local rivalry, in which Cornwall abounds. To prevent the hake from ravaging the mackerel stocks, the St Ives fishermen were supposed to have caught a large hake, whipped it, then put it back into the sea to warn off its fellows. The story was popularly attributed to Zennor men: the St Ives reply was the story of Zennor men building a wall around a cuckoo so that it would always be spring.

Page 36. *The vicar of St Ives says ...* The most often quoted anecdote in the Cornish Diary. Kilvert must have been told this story by the Hockins at Phillack: he never went to St Ives. The vicar concerned was John Balmer Jones, whom the Hockins knew well: he was curate of St Ives 1863–6, then curate of Phillack 1868–9, before returning to St Ives as vicar in 1869. All visitors to St Ives agreed on the violent smell of fish which pervaded the town from the pilchard industry. Typical is the comment of W.G. Maton some seventy-five years earlier: 'The stench arising from the stores, and from the putrid *rejectamenta* lying about the town, is to strangers almost intolerable' ('Observations on the Western Counties of England, 1794–96', in *Early Tours in Devon and Cornwall*, edited by R. Pearse Chope, 1918; reprinted Newton Abbot, 1967, p.260). Similarly Bottrell, describing a visitor to St Ives, refers to 'the sickening smells, and stunning odours of the very essence of stench, which saluted him at every turn, as he picked his way through the Digey, and leaped the gutters about Charn Chy. It was in the midst of a busy fishery season ...' (p.52). The old town in Kilvert's time was still heavily dependent on the pilchard industry, and unattractive to visitors – Bottrell calls it 'the old dirty town under the hill' (p.13). But above the town, on the eastern side overlooking Porthminster Sands where the air was purer, lodging houses had recently been built and bathing machines were available for summer guests.

Page 37. *We did not know it ...* George Gregory, 19, of Lelant, a worker at the Hayle Foundry, was drowned shortly after eleven o'clock while bathing near the Foundry Pool; the body was not found until 1.30 p.m. There is a detailed report in the *West Briton* on Tuesday 26 July. Given Kilvert's inaccurate information, one wonders when and how he did hear of the tragedy.

Page 38. *Market Jew* The novelist Mrs Craik expressed a very similar reaction on her visit a few years later: 'We entered Marazion; – and found it, despite its picturesque name, the most commonplace little town imaginable!', *An Unsentimental Journey Through Cornwall* (London, 1884, p.98).

Page 39. *the famous Beacon ...* The Chair was indeed the medieval lighthouse cresset. The quote is from Macaulay's *The Armada*:

> For swift to east and swift to west the ghastly war-flame spread,
> High on St Michael's Mount it shone: it shone on Beachy Head.

Page 41. *The signatures of the Queen ...* The Royal visit was on 28 July 1865.

Page 41. *A man was bathing ...* The man would have been naked at this date. Mrs Craik observed a similar sight in Mount's Bay: 'Toilette in an open boat was evidently the custom of the country' (*An Unsentimental Journey*, p.101).

Page 42. *searching for ferns ...* This notebook is full of allusions to the Victorian mania for collecting ferns, which prompted a whole literature of fern books. Emma Hockin was clearly a passionate collector; it is interesting to note that after they had to leave Tullimaar, the Hockins ran a nursery garden in Taunton and called their house The Ferns.

Page 42. *Miss Emily and Miss Charlotte Hockin* They were daughters of Williams Hockin, solicitor, of Strangways Terrace, Truro, and cousins to H. Emily was 28 and Charlotte 18.

Page 43. *Mary Mundy a genuine Cornish Celt ...* This seems to be the earliest of several literary references to Mary Mundy, who was clearly a considerable character. She first became well known five years later thanks to the vicar of Mullion, Edmund George Harvey, whose endearing local history *Mullyon* (Truro and London, 1875) – known as the 'Gull Book' from the large gull on the cover – contains anonymous extracts in her honour from the Old Inn Visitors' Book. These consist of two Latin epigrams, a piece in Greek, and an 84-line doggerel poem in English, all dated between October 1870 and April 1874, and in fact written by the good-humoured eccentric John Stuart Blackie, Professor of Greek at Edinburgh. There-

after Mary Mundy featured in guide books. Mrs Craik has a great deal to say about her, and her impressions agree closely with Kilvert's (*An Unsentimental Journey*, pp.36, 40–4). She describes her as she was in the early 1880s: 'She stood at the door to greet us – a bright, brown-faced little woman with the reddest of cheeks and the blackest of eyes ... a regular stream of chatty conversation, given in the strongest Cornish, with the kindliest of Cornish hearts ... her talk was so shrewd and her looks so pleasant – once, no doubt, actually pretty, and still comely enough for a middle-aged woman'.

Page 44. *the Church has been nicely restored ...* The restoration was only completed in 1870. There is a full description in Harvey's *Mullyon*, pp.27–30.

Page 44. *We went to the Rectory ...* Harvey had been vicar of Mullion since 1865. The Hockin sisters probably knew him from the time when he was rector of St Mary's, Truro, 1860–5. The lifeboat station had been opened in 1867.

Page 44. *Lady's Finger* The name is used for both *Lotus corniculatus* (bird's foot trefoil) and *Anthyllis vulneraria* (kidney vetch). Both grow on the Lizard peninsula, although neither would have been found in a wheatfield; but a passage such as this is best seen in terms of an Impressionist painting rather than an exact botanical description.

Page 45. *the cormorants black and evil-looking ...* Here, and in a passage just below ('two black cormorants flew overhead going inland like two devils'), Kilvert has in mind a dramatic passage in *Paradise Lost* describing Satan:

Thence up he flew, and on the Tree of Life,
The middle Tree and highest there that grew,
Sat like a Cormorant ... (IV, 194–8)

Page 45. *Polurrian* Kilvert actually wrote 'Felurrian', here and a few lines later, presumably misreading his own rough notes when writing up his diary.

Page 46. *large long-horned cows ...* Not 'Spanish cattle' but South Devons, very popular cattle in nineteenth-century Cornwall. They were a true dual-purpose breed, providing good beef and rich milk that many people still think is unsurpassed for making clotted cream.

Page 46. *"croft"* The local usage of the word is defined in M.A. Courtney, *A Glossary of Words in Use in West Cornwall* (1880) as: 'an enclosed common not yet cultivated'. The usage is still current.

Page 47. *the palace of the Nereids* the sea-nymphs of Greek mythology.

Page 47. *the hoof of the learned Erasmus* A baffling joke! Pegasus, favourite steed of the Muses, caused the fountain Hippocrene to well forth on Mount Helicon with a stroke of his hoof; but the connection between this and the sixteenth-century humanist scholar is obscure to say the least. It seems a mistake to look for recondite scholarly allusions when Kilvert and H. are bantering around: the point of the joke probably lies in its very silliness.

Page 48. *"hedges"* Kilvert has already described the Cornish hedges on Hayle Towans. They were a particular feature of the Lizard: in the 1920s Mullion people still referred to Lizard people as 'Lizard hedgers' (information from Mrs Jane Tregoning, former teacher at Mullion school).

Page 48. *Landewednack* Kilvert wrote 'Llandewednack', slipping into Welsh spelling. He left a large space within the parentheses, and did not completely fill it when he added the three names.

Page 49. *the Lizard people are of Spanish descent ...* cf. C.A. Johns, *A Week at the Lizard* (London, 1848, revised edn 1873): 'Tradition asserts that the Lizard was at some very remote period colonized by Spanish emigrants. There is still something very Spanish about the features and complexion of many of the inhabitants' (p.48). This 'tradition' is not confined to the Lizard: many families in West Cornwall preserve a legend of 'Spanish blood', not all originating in sixteenth-century coastal raids!

Page 49. *"low splendour"* From Tennyson's 'The Marriage of Geraint', *Idylls of the King*, lines 597–8:

But when the third day from the hunting-morn
Made a low splendour in the world ...

Kilvert here applies the phrase to sunset, but in an entry for Thursday 2 June 1870 (*NLW 1*, p.74) he uses it more appropriately for sunrise.

Page 50. *a stuffed Cornish Chough* Kilvert is echoing a general concern felt at the time over the survival of Cornwall's national bird, a concern which did not inhibit the popularity of collecting stuffed or live specimens. The *West Briton* reported on 14 April 1870 that the latest price for choughs had risen to as much as £3.10s a pair; the same month the *Cornish Telegraph* noted their extreme rarity, and suggested that breeding in the Scillies was the only hope to save them from complete extinction. They struggled on for a further century on the north coast: the last solitary wild native Cornish chough died about 1970 at Beacon Cove just north of Newquay.

Page 51. *Carclew* One of the finest houses and estates in Cornwall. Carclew was built in 1728, and the deer park and plantations extended to over a square mile. It was long owned by the Lemon family. The house was burnt down on 5 April 1934.

Page 51. *Dora* Kilvert's sister. She must have already visited Tullimaar, presumably before the Diary begins in early 1870.

Page 51. *"I know a bank ..."* The correct quotation is of course 'I know a bank whereon the wild thyme blows' (*Midsummer Night's Dream*, II, 1).

Page 52. *The Chancel is restored* The chancel of St Piran's Church was rebuilt in 1841–2; but the present church shows the effects of a typically drastic St Aubyn restoration of 1884–5. The private walk from Tullimaar is now closed. The clergyman was Edward Hawkins, curate of Perranarworthal 1858–75, and then in his mid-forties.

Page 53. *"Aside the devil turned ..."* A startling reference in this context: one of the most intimately self-revealing notes in the whole of the Diary as we have it. It probably only survived the successive censorings after Kilvert's death because of its obliqueness. The reference is to *Paradise Lost*, Book IV, after an evocative and sensual description of the unrestrained mutual love of Adam and Eve:

aside the Devil turned
For envy, yet with jealous leer malign
Eyed them askance, and to himself thus plained:
    Sight hateful, sight tormenting! thus these two
Imparadised in one another's arms
The happier *Eden*, shall enjoy their fill
Of bliss on bliss, while I to Hell am thrust,
Where neither joy nor love, but fierce desire,
Among our other torments not the least,
Still unfulfilled with pain of longing pines ...

Page 53. *a fern owl* The short-eared owl (also sometimes the nightjar).

Page 53. *a great high picturesque old draw well* The top of the well has now been removed. The wisteria on the gardener's house has also gone, although its base can still be seen.

Page 53. *Emily's wedding day* The wedding anniversary of Kilvert's sister. He also notes the day in the Diary on Thursday 25 July 1872.

Page 53. *Bottrell* See the note to Thursday 21 July. Bottrell describes himself as an 'An Old Celt' on the title-page of his work. Kilvert makes several subsequent references to it.

Page 54. *Martin the groom* James Martin was 31, and lived on the Tullimaar estate with his wife and two small children.

Page 54. *"Redruth Kings"* Local rivalries again: the 'joke and reproach' was particularly levelled by Camborne people. The event was supposed to have happened at the coronation of George IV, or in other versions that of William IV.

Page 55. *"sawns"* Usually spelt 'zawn': in West Penwith both would have been pronounced the same. Bottrell uses both spellings in his tale of Giant Wrath of Portreath, Kilvert's source.

Page 56. *the St Ives lifeboat men* This could refer to any one of half a dozen episodes of extraordinary heroism by the St Ives lifeboat between 1865 and 1870. The little boat *Moses* and later *Moses II* would struggle across to Lelant, Hayle Bar, Hell's Mouth and Portreath, constantly overturning in the wild seas, and effect rescues that seem almost incredible today. See for example Cyril Noall and Grahame Farr, *Wreck and Rescue Round the Cornish Coast: The Story of the Land's End lifeboats* (Truro, 1965), pp.18–21, 41.

Page 56. *I was sorry I could not see it ...* Kilvert had a certain weakness of sight that he felt keenly. He often refers to it in the Diary; and yet he was able to see the seal at Gwithian a few days later.

Page 57. *a fine race between four pilot boats ...* Kilvert's boat numbers do not tally with the report in the *West Briton* on Thursday 28 July, but do match those given in the *Falmouth Packet* on Saturday 30 July. His general account of this exciting race is strikingly accurate and vivid. The boats in finishing order were *Antelope*, 41 tons, *Vie*, 43 tons, *Richard Green*, 46 tons, and *Alarm*, 46 tons. The *West Briton* gave the *Antelope*'s weight as 58 tons and reported, like the diarist, that the lighter *Vie* was awarded the first prize (of £15); but the *Packet* corrects this: 'The *Antelope* was entered as 58 tons, but on referring to her register at the Custom House, on the following day, it was found that she was only 41 tons.' Thus Kilvert could not have 'written up' his description later from either of the newspaper reports.

Page 59. *Three candles were burning ...* Miss M.A. Courtney describes this superstition in her *Cornish Feasts and Folk-Lore* (Penzance, 1890), p.165: 'Three candles burning at the same time is the sign of a wedding; and the girl who is nearest to the door, the cupboard, and the shortest candle, will be married first'. Kilvert was very interested in such proverbial sayings and local customs and traditions, and it is known that he compiled a substantial manuscript collection of Radnorshire material. This was used by his niece Essex Smith as the base for an article in the *Occult Review* in September 1921, but she later destroyed the manuscripts as she did most of the Diary.

Page 60. *Capt. and Mrs Parker and Miss Lewis* Kilvert does not hint at the extraordinary situation prevailing at Rosewarne, an impressive early nineteenth-century house in large grounds. Rosewarne had been owned by the immensely wealthy Mrs Mary Hartley, a lunatic, and after she accidentally burnt herself to death in 1868 it passed to her son William Henry Harris Hartley, also a lunatic (both descriptions from the Census returns). The Court of Chancery appointed family connections as 'Committees' to care for the Hartleys and manage their estates: the Parkers had lived at Rosewarne in this capacity since 1864, and Miss Lewis's father, the Revd William Price Lewis, had similarly lived there as Chaplain and 'Committee' until his early death in 1853. Captain Frederick Townley Parker, a well-connected man of considerable qualities, was 38 in 1870, and Mrs Parker (Louisa Elizabeth

Katherine, née Little) was 36. Mary Augusta Lewis was 26. Both families had close connections with the Welsh border gentry, and it seems likely that Kilvert's initial acquaintance with them came through his vicar, the Revd Venables, rather than through the Hockins. The whole bizarre and complex situation at Rosewarne, and the admirable roles acted by Kilvert's friends, has been unravelled by Barry Smith: 'Rosewarne, the Parkers and the Lewises – Insanity, Imbecility and Inter-relationships in a Victorian Family', *Kilvert Society Newsletter* (September 1984), pp.7–12.

Rosewarne passed to a distant relative after William Hartley's death in 1894. In 1911 it was bought by the Holman family, founders of Holman Brothers, the famous Camborne engineering company; it subsequently became the Company's head office. Rosewarne is now the Gladys Holman Home for Spastics.

Page 60. *we turned inland by the Church* ... Kilvert left the church's name blank; a few lines earlier he had left the name of the hotel blank, and filled in 'Western' later. His account of this road can be compared with that in J.T. Blight, *A Week at the Land's End* (quoted from the 2nd edn, 1876): 'The beautifully wooded grounds of Trereife, about a mile from the town, first attract attention; the roadway is here arched with a long avenue of noble elms; near its extremity it is crossed by another avenue ... On the ascent of a hill, a little beyond Trereife, an old oak forms a complete archway over the road, and if you are on the seat of the carriage beside the driver, he will probably tell you that it is the only instance of the kind to be met with on the journey from London to the Land's End. A short distance from this, on the left hand side of the road, stands an ancient cross ...' (pp.58–9).

Page 61. *"Proceed Edward"* Edward for a donkey, rather than the common Neddy, is quite frequently found in West Cornwall, although unlike Neddy not given in *The Oxford English Dictionary*. The joke depended, of course, on the driver Edward Noy recognizing it immediately.

Page 62. *Buryan* Kilvert wrote 'Buryan' and 'Burian' within two sentences.

Page 62. *"crows"* An old Cornish word for a shed, sty, hovel, etc, still in use for a small farm building housing animals (cf. the Welsh *crau*, a sty).

Page 63. *[Porth Curnow]* Kilvert left the name blank, and it has been filled in later in pencil by a different hand, most likely by Kilvert's sister Dora. The hand seems to be the same as that which filled in 'The Royal Cornwall Sailors' Home' earlier.

Pages 63–4. *Lieutenant Goldsmith* The commander of a revenue cutter, and nephew of Oliver Goldsmith, he tipped the Logan Stone down the rocks on 8 April 1824. His motive was probably to disprove William Borlase's confident claim that 'the extremities of its base are at such a distance from each other, and so well secured by their nearness to the Stone, which it stretches itself upon, that it is morally impossible that any lever, or indeed any force (however applied in a mechanical way), can remove it from its present situation' (*Antiquities Historical and Monumental of the County of Cornwall*, 2nd edn (London, 1769), p.180). He was obliged by the Admiralty to replace it at his own expense; Davies Gilbert, the Cornish President of the Royal Society, gave £25 to help the project. The rock was replaced on 2 November 1824. As early as 1842, Cyrus Redding was complaining about the commercialization of the Logan Stone resulting from all the publicity ('the notoriety of what the good officer did, has produced the common result of turning it into a money-show', *An Illustrated Itinerary of the County of Cornwall* (London, 1842), p.181).

Page 64. *grinning like dogs* Psalm 59, v.6, on 'them that offend of malicious wickedness': 'They go to and fro in the evening: they grin like a dog, and run about through the city'.

Page 64. *a paradise of black pigs* The village is Treen. These Land's End parishes had pigs of character. W.H. Hudson commented: 'It is pleasant to see the pigs in these parts, as they are allowed more liberty in the fields and about the house than they usually get in other places', in *The Land's End* (2nd edn 1911), p.33; and P.A.S. Pool notes of a neighbouring parish that 'Sancreed parish has for centuries been famous for its pigs; indeed its inhabitants were long known jocularly to their neighbours as "Sancreed pigs"' (*A Cornish Farmer's Diary* [James Stevens of Zennor and Sancreed, 1847–1918], edited by P.A.S. Pool (Penzance, 1977, p.19).

Page 64. *"the Landmarks"* 'Conspicuous objects on the high ground above Tol-pedn are two landmarks or beacons; one is painted red, the other black and white; they are about twelve feet high, and are placed in a line with a dangerous rock called the Runnel Stone, which lies about a mile from the shore, and has been fatal to many vessels' (Blight, *A Week at the Land's End*, 1876 edn, p.106).

Page 65. *A young man was once caught ...* Blight tells what is probably the original of this story: 'Some time ago,

two gentlemen from the eastern part of the kingdom entered the cavern without being acquainted with the tides, and having lingered too long within, when they came to the entrance the sea had formed a barrier to the ledge on the opposite side which it was necessary to gain. It was truly an awful situation ... Fortunately, one of them could swim, and managed to get across, and hastened to the nearest dwelling for assistance to his luckless companion ... After remaining in this state of suspense and terror for some time, a welcome shout is heard above – his friend has returned with some fishermen, who, by the use of ropes, draw him safely to the summit' (pp.109–10).

Page 66. *"cape beyond cape"* From Macaulay's *The Armada*:

> Far on the deep the Spaniard saw, along each south-
> ern shire,
> Cape beyond cape, in endless range, those twin-
> kling points of fire.

Page 66. *the Lighthouse on the Wolf Rock* This lighthouse was new, and not yet working. It was built from 1861 to 1869, but did not start operating until January 1871. The bell buoy was probably that laid on the Runnelstone in 1825 (by Lieutenant Goldsmith of the revenue cutter *Nimble*, the villain of the Logan Stone), although this buoy frequently broke loose and had to be replaced. It is surprising that Kilvert does not mention the famous Longships lighthouse, built in 1795. Several pages of the notebook here consist of isolated paragraphs with blank spaces in between, while the entries on the different rocks etc. do not follow any particular order (the Dollar Rock, for example, is much further on, close to Land's End), and there are other unexpected omissions. Kilvert is clearly jotting down details as he remembers them, and leaving space for possible amplification or further details.

Page 66. *another Logan Rock* The one at Pendower Cove: known as Bosistow Logan Rock, being on Bosistow Cliff.

Page 67. *the "Irish Lady"* This brief mention is out of place here: the rock is the far side of Land's End. It is very curious that, having noted the Irish Lady, Kilvert does not tell the legend associated with the rock, which he must have read or been told, and which seems just the sort to appeal to him; perhaps he intended to add it later, with this note as a reminder. Robert Hunt includes it in his *Popular Romances of the West of England*: 'Near Pedn-men-dw ... is a curiously-shaped rock, known as the Irish Lady. In days long ago some adventurous sailors from Ireland were shipwrecked at night on this rock, and every soul perished, save a lady, who was seen in the morning sitting on the top of the rock. The storm was still raging, and it was quite impossible to render this solitary sufferer any assistance. Days and nights passed away; the people watched the dying woman from the shore, but they could not reach her. At length they saw that her sufferings were at an end; and at last the dead body was washed into the sea' (3rd edn, 1881, p.183). Hunt dates the event to the reign of Charles I. Sir Humphry Davy, poet as well as scientist, introduced the legend into an unfinished poem on Mount's Bay written in 1795–6 (*The Poetry of Humphry Davy*, edited by Alison Pritchard (Penzance, 1978, pp.5–6). Blight also tells it briefly (p.94).

Page 67. *the magnificence of the lichens* cf. Blight at Funnel Cavern: 'the rocks are thickly spread with lichens and moss; yellow, orange, and green are beautifully blended. Indeed if an artist were to paint it as it appears, it might be thought he had daubed his picture with all the colours of his palette merely for a gay effect' (p.111).

Page 67. *an old tin-stamping wheel* Kilvert is now in the cove called Nanjizal or Mill Bay, just beyond Bosistow Logan Rock and about a mile from Land's End. Zawn Pyg forms the southern boundary of the cove, the remains of the old Nanjizal Mine and stamps are by the stream in the middle, and the Scilly Cable telegraph house was at Zawn Reeve Cove at the northern end. This cable had finally been laid as recently as September 1869; there is an item in the *West Briton* for Tuesday 26 July 1870 – the day before Kilvert's visit – on the useful work that it was doing.

Page 67. *the old Cornish giants* A reminiscence of the description in Bottrell of the construction of the 'giants' hedges', 'built with such large rocks as no ten men of these days can lift' (p.15).

Page 68. *a "duke"* A variety of cherry. This joke has been added at the bottom of the page as an afterthought.

Page 69. *the great cavern* cf. Blight: 'A large cavern, called the Land's End Hole, in Cornish, Vau-Laz, about a hundred and fifty feet in length, runs directly through the promontory, and can be got at during low water, under the direction of a guide; the sea flows through it, and it is said that boats have passed from one side to the other; but it seems too narrow in the middle, and had it been wide enough, the sea must be very calm indeed to permit such a feat' (p.74).

Page 70. *the insufferable snobs* The *OED* defines this older use of 'snob' as: 'One who has little or no breeding or good taste; a vulgar or ostentatious person'. Even at this time, about a hundred tourists a day were visiting Land's End.

Page 70. *the first mile stone* Wilkie Collins had had the same thought when he visited Land's End in 1850: 'He [the stranger] will observe ... an old milestone marked "I", and will be informed that this is the real original first mile in England; as if all measurement of distance began strictly from the West!' (*Rambles Beyond Railways*, reprint of 1861 edn (London, 1982), p.97).

Page 71. *Market Jew Chapel* The Independent or Congregationalist chapel was built in 1707 and rebuilt in 1807. The remains of four infants had been discovered on Tuesday 19 July, and the inquest the next day was reported in the *West Briton* on 26 July, and more fully in the *Cornish Telegraph* on 27 July, the day of Kilvert's visit. Three at least were thought possibly to have been stillborn, while the fourth and largest had, pathetically, been carefully dressed in beautiful clothes. It was suggested that they might have been placed above the ceiling (not 'stuffed into holes and corners') twenty or thirty years earlier by the then sexton; but the mystery was never fully resolved. A verdict of 'Found dead' was returned.

Page 71. *the handsomest in Cornwall* Innumerable visitors commented on the beauty of the young women of West Penwith, and Penzance girls in particular seem to have had an almost legendary reputation. Many writers had clearly studied them closely. Thus Cyrus Redding noted that 'some of the girls of these villages are very pretty ... all are round in the limbs, and walk with a mixture of elasticity and firmness; erect in their carriage, and the form admirably developed' (*An Illustrated Itinerary*,

1842, pp.168–9); while a generation earlier the Revd Richard Warner had admired their beauty and freshness, their smooth delicate skin, rounded figures and healthy colour, and attributed their 'plumpness of form and delicacy of the external cuticle' to the fact that they ate so many pilchards! (*A Tour Through Cornwall in the Autumn of 1808*, pp.152–3). F.W.L. Stockdale, describing Penzance, wrote enigmatically: 'This town has long been noted for the pleasantness of its situation, the salubrity of its air, and the beauty of its natives; and is in consequence much resorted to by travellers, who, in most instances, have derived more benefit than they had anticipated' (*Excursions in the County of Cornwall*, 1824, p.59).

Page 72. *the hostess* Presumably Joanna Phillips Hockin, wife of Williams Hockin, solicitor of Truro, and aunt by marriage to H.

Page 72. *St Michael Pen Kevil* The restoration, by George Edmund Street, had been undertaken in 1862–5.

Page 72. *heavy cake* This Cornish speciality, a plain cake or bun containing currants, would have been new to Kilvert, as were pasties the previous week. Heavy cake originated in the fishing towns, and is supposed to have gained its name from the look-out huer's cry of *hevva!* (the Cornish word for a shoal of fish) when a shoal of pilchards was seen. The housewives made the cake then, to provide something to eat for the next few days when all hands would be busy cleaning and salting the pilchards.

Page 73. *Charmeth she wisely?* The reference is to Psalm 58, verse 4: 'Even like the deaf adder that stoppeth her ears; which refuseth to hear the voice of the charmer: charm he never so wisely' (Prayer Book version).

Page 73. *Agatha* Agatha Hockin was 14. She lived until 1936, and Barry Smith has spoken to people who remember her: interestingly, in the light of Kilvert's subsequent comments, she is recalled as having been 'odd in the head', although she was of course very old by then.

Page 73. *Old Kea* Kilvert actually wrote 'Old Quay'. He had left a space for the name, which he put in later. He heard the name accurately, but was not aware of the correct spelling.

Page 73. *"the stately ships ..."* From Tennyson's *Break, break, break*:

And the stately ships go on
  To their haven under the hill;
But O for the touch of a vanished hand,
  And the sound of a voice that is still!

Page 74. *St Ives Consols* The richest and most extensive mine in the entire area, which produced 16,400 tons of black tin between 1827 and 1892. 'Now its only remains are a few granite blocks, a wheel pit or two and the counthouse' (A.C. Todd and Peter Laws, *Industrial Archaeology of Cornwall*, 1972, p.69). The mine was situated near the junction of the present B3306 and B3311 roads: there were steam stamps opposite Consols Farm, and water-wheel stamps in Hellesveor Moor and on the site of the little reservoir on Bussow Moor. Details are given in A.K. Hamilton Jenkin, *Mines and Miners of Cornwall: I. Around St Ives* (1961, reprinted Bracknell, 1978), pp.20–1, and Cyril Noall, *The St Ives Mining District* (1982). It would indeed have been easier for Kilvert's party to have gone through Towednack on the other side of Rosewall Hill.

Page 74. *a notorious country for giants* Bottrell's first collection of tales – among the most delightful and evocative in his book – is called 'The Giants of Towednack' (pp.9–46).

Page 75. *seven wives and all* In the context, the humorous reference has an extra dimension. Kilvert has at the back of his mind Bottrell's tale of 'The Piskey-Led Commercial Traveller's Ride over the Hills', whose starting-point is the old rhyme: prompted by a life-long curiosity, a traveller from Birmingham rides over from Penzance to visit St Ives and tries to imagine where the man with seven wives might have lived; but on the way back, he becomes hopelessly lost in the maze of lanes in the hills, an ominous precedent for Kilvert's party.

Page 76. *"fragments of forgotten peoples ..."* From Tennyson's 'The Passing of Arthur' in the *Idylls of the King*:

Then rose the King and moved his host by night,
And ever push'd Sir Modred, league by league,
Back to the sunset bound of Lyonnesse —
A land of old upheaven from the abyss
By fire, to sink into the abyss again;
Where fragments of forgotten peoples dwelt,
And the long mountains ended in a coast
Of ever-shifting sand, and far away
The phantom circle of a moaning sea. (lines 79–87)

Page 76. *a Captain — had fallen ...* The accident happened on Wednesday 4 May 1870: the victim was Captain Thomas Opie, 49, manager of the English Arsenic Co. at Roseworthy. The owner and driver of the omnibus was John Martin, who ran a service on Wednesdays from Camborne to Truro and back. Capt. Opie was travelling from Redruth to Camborne, sitting on the front seat by the driver, when he fell off going down Blowing-House Hill and the wheel went over his head. He died on the Friday morning, 6 May. Full details are given in the *West Briton* of 5 May, 10 May, and 12 May (report of the inquest).

Page 77.   *she did not despise mine*   Indeed, when Kilvert visited the Hockins in Taunton in September 1872, he recorded: 'Mrs Hockin gave me what I valued extremely, one of the plants of *Asplenium Marinum* fern which I got for her at the Gurnard's Head two years ago and which she has kept ever since' (Saturday, 14 September 1872, *Kilvert's Diary* II, p.268).

Page 77.   *scrambling like goats and conies*   Psalm 104, verse 18: 'The high hills are a refuge for the wild goats; and the rocks for the conies.'

Page 77.   *a small ancient chapel*   Known as Chapel Jane, and dating from the twelfth or thirteenth century. The ruins are on the edge of the cliff above Treen cove on the eastern side of Gurnard's Head.

Page 78.   *their school 2 miles off*   Perhaps the National (Church) School at Zennor Churchtown. The building is now used as a village hall.

Page 78.   *her brother has lately taken ...*   Mrs Parker did not have a brother: the new tenant of Bronllys was her half-sister's husband, William Clode Braddon. No doubt she simplified the relationship in dinner-party conversation. Mrs Parker herself lived at Llanvair Grange, Llanvair Kilgeddin, Monmouthshire, at the time of her marriage.

Page 78.   *hung round with horns ...*   The trophies were last seen in the attic at Holman Brothers' old works in Camborne. No-one knows what has become of them.

Page 78.   *Daylight had not appeared*   'We won't go home till morning, till daylight doth appear!' (chorus of popular song).

Page 79.   *This morning we met two girls*   Added as an afterthought on a third of a page left blank at the end of the day's entry. They must have met the girls when setting out for Rosewarne.

Page 80.   *the gardener*   Richard Tresidder was 56. He had been gardener at Tullimaar for many years: he was already living in the cottage with his wife Ann at the time of the 1851 census.

Page 80.   *Addie Cholmeley*   Born 31 July 1854, daughter of Adelaide (née Kilvert), the diarist's cousin, and Mountague Cholmeley, of Wainfleet, Lincs. It was at Addie's wedding on 11 August 1874 that Kilvert met Katherine Mary Heanley ('Kathleen Mavourneen' of the Diary) and fell in love with her.

Page 80.   *illustrated by Doré*   The magnificent edition with Doré's engravings was published in London in 1868.

Page 81.   *The owl and the baker's daughter*   The quote is from *Hamlet*, IV, 5, spoken by Ophelia when deranged (correctly: ' ... Lord, we know what we are ...'). It refers to a legend in which Christ went into a baker's shop and asked for bread. The baker's daughter rebuked her mother for giving him too much, and was promptly turned into an owl. However, one wonders how far Kilvert and

Emma Hockin pursued their discussion, since Ophelia's own explanation for her remark, which follows immediately, is anything but decorous:

... when they ask you what it means, say you this:
 To-morrow is Saint Valentine's day,
  All in the morning betime,
 And I a maid at your window,
  To be your Valentine.
 Then up he rose, and donn'd his clothes,
  And dupped the chamber door,
 Let in the maid, that out a maid
  Never departed more ...

... By Gis, and by Saint Charity,
  Alack, and fie for shame:
 Young men will do't, if they come to't,
  By Cock they are to blame.
 Quoth she, before you tumbled me,
  You promis'd me to wed.
 So would I ha' done by yonder sun,
  And thou hadst not come to my bed.

Equally, it would be interesting to know which part of *Othello* they discussed.

Page 81. *The escape from drowning* There seems to be no way of knowing to what this might refer. On 27 April 1870, when visiting his friends the Dews in Whitney-on-Wye, Kilvert had read a letter from young Arthur Dew, who was serving as a naval cadet on HMS *Liverpool*, and had written from Auckland in February. He comments that the letter is 'well written and amusing' (*NLW 1*, p.2), and this note might possibly refer to some anecdote in it. The papers also carried occasional newsletters from New Zealand (the most recent in *The Times* being Thursday 28 July), but nothing has yet come to light that explains the remark. It is more likely, though, that it relates to something that Kilvert has just been told. Emma Hockin had connections with New Zealand: her parents had lived there in the early 1840s, and she herself seems to have been born on board ship during the journey back to England in 1844.

Page 81. *Polonius to Laertes* From *Hamlet*, I, 3. Again a slight misquotation: it should read ' ... with hoops of steel'.

Page 81. *"Here's to the devil ..."* From Bottrell's story of 'Betty Toddy and her Gown'. At St Just Feast, 'many a merry jig and three-handed reel was kept agoing by the tune being sung to such old catches as

 Here's to the devil,
 With his wooden spade and shovel,
 Digging tin by the bushel,
  With his tail cocked up' (p.144)

The song also figures (with the second line 'With his wooden pick and shovel') in Robert Hunt's *Popular Romances of the West of England*, in the tale of 'Duffy and the Devil' (1881 edn, p.245).

Page 84. *What is the meaning of those holes?* They are of course for the most part slots for roof trusses. The ivy has been cleared away, but otherwise Kilvert's description is strikingly accurate of the castle as it appears today.

Page 85. *Happily we were uninterrupted* This passage, not printed by Plomer, helps explain Kilvert's frequently expressed loathing of noisy tourists. It was not simply a matter of social class, although that might at times (but not always) have come into it. Rather it was a question of intrusion: Kilvert loved to project himself imaginatively into a scene of old ruins or natural beauty, and strongly resented it when the Wordsworthian spell was broken.

Page 86. *some steep pitches* 'pitch' is a Radnorshire word meaning 'a steep hill', which Kilvert often uses; see W.E.T. Morgan, *Radnorshire Words* (English Dialect Society Series, no. 32, 1881).

Page 86. *Lanhydrock* This was the old Lanhydrock, built in the seventeenth century and one of the grandest houses in Cornwall. All except one wing was burnt down in 1881, but rebuilt in a similar style.

Page 86. *Lord Robarts* the spelling is in fact 'Robartes'.

Page 86. *a lofty monument* General Sir Walter Raleigh Gilbert (1785–1853), of Indian army fame, was born in Bodmin. His monument on Beacon Hill is 144 feet high.

Page 88. *Bowithick* Kilvert actually wrote 'Bowilick'.

Page 88. *Mr G. Venables* George Stovin Venables, QC (1810–88), brother of Kilvert's vicar the Revd Richard Venables. He was a highly gifted man with many literary friends: the *DNB* says that 'he was almost without an equal in the extraordinary force and charm of his character'; and on his journalism: 'he was one of the original contributors to the *Saturday Review*, in the first number of which (1 November 1855) he wrote the first leading article. From that date until very shortly before his death he contributed an article or two to that paper almost every week, and he probably did more than any other writer of his time to establish and maintain the best and strongest current style, and the highest type of political thought, in journalism.'

Page 88. *Mr Cook of the Saturday Review* John Douglas Cook (1808?–68), sometime editor of the *Morning Chronicle* and founder-editor of the *Saturday Review*. He built Trevena House, now the front part of 'King Arthur's Hall', and came to Tintagel every summer in the 1860s. Emma Hardy, the novelist's wife, described his visits in her memoirs: 'There was a great and important visitor in the village of Tintagel, who came periodically every summer, Mr Cook the then Editor of the Saturday Review ... Poultry was fatted for him, weeks before, a cook kept expressly at the little Inn for him, fish sent from London daily and his dinner nightly was considered a very banquet to which he invited invariably only the clergyman, Mr Kinsman', in *Some Recollections*, eds Evelyn Hardy and Robert Gittings (London, 1961), p.41; see A.C. Canner, *The Parish of Tintagel: Some Historical Notes* (n.p., 1982), p.85.

Page 90. *the old man usually sends his daughter* Canner mentions the mill tenant's daughter, Florence Nightingale Richards, who 'continued for many years until extreme old age to escort parties of visitors round the Island' (*The Parish of Tintagel*, p.86).

Page 90. *They have just begun mining* 'It is strange to think of the castle precincts being invaded by industrial concerns. But in 1870 blasting was causing anxiety, and by 1880 a silver-lead mine was in operation' (Canner, *The parish of Tintagel*, p.86). The mine later failed.

Page 90. *"Upon the sands ..."* The quotation is from 'Guinevere' in the *Idylls of the King*:

For there was no man knew from whence he came;
But after tempest, when the long wave broke
All down the thundering shores of Bude and Bos,
There came a day as still as Heaven, and then
They found a naked child upon the sands
Of wild Dundagil by the Cornish sea;
And that was Arthur ...

Interestingly, Kilvert is not quoting from the Doré edition (1868), which reads 'Of dark Dundagil ...', but he correctly gives Tennyson's first version of the line. The revision was made in the 1860s; Tennyson later changed the line again to 'dark Tintagil'.

Page 91. *The "saddle bits"* Presumably the top of the battlements.

Page 92. *A broad slab ...* Cf. C.A. Ralegh Radford, *Tintagel Castle* (Department of the Environment Official Handbook, HMSO, 18th impression, 1979; first published 1935): 'At the east end the altar has been rebuilt, but the granite slab was found on the site during the nineteenth century' (p.29).

Page 92. *... beautifully carved with the quatre foil* Ralegh Radford does not mention any carved stone, but only notes that 'two fragments of a small slate headstone with an incised Maltese cross have been found among the debris of the chapel' (p.34). The account of the site has been updated and considerably revised in line with the most recent knowledge in Charles Thomas's *Tintagel Castle* (London: English Heritage, 1986). This says of the chapel: 'The large granite base of the altar top, replaced at the east end, and parts of a slate front panel for the altar with a cross incised on it, should be several centuries older than the Castle' (p.12), but also does not mention any carved stone. The answer to the riddle of what Kilvert saw is probably provided by Canner: 'The chapel was not devoid of ornament: carved stones have been found among the ruins, one of which, triangular in shape and enclosing a "marigold" design, is now set in the centre of the Lady chapel altar in the parish church' (*The Parish of Tintagel*, p.11).

Page 93. *"mist clung like a face cloth ..."* From Tennyson's 'Guinevere', lines 5–8:

> ... for all abroad,
> Beneath a moon unseen albeit at full,
> The white mist, like a face-cloth to the face,
> Clung to the dead earth, and the land was still.

The quotation adds a morbid note that is in keeping with Kilvert's sensibility, but hardly seems to be suggested by the rest of the afternoon.

Page 93. *Tintagel Church* The church was being restored at the time, another Cornish victim of the architect J. Piers St Aubyn's zeal. The grand re-opening was on 11 October 1870. John Douglas Cook died in 1868 and was buried in the isolated churchyard; there is a stained-glass window to his memory in the church. The Revd Richard Byrn Kinsman was vicar of Tintagel from 1851 to 1894. He was a gifted and versatile polymath of a type familiar in Victorian country parishes, and did a great deal to preserve the castle as well as the church (see Canner, *The Parish of Tintagel*, pp.85–7). Kilvert had left a space for his name and filled it in later.

Page 94. *the "Flying Dutchman"* The train started in 1862, running from London to Penzance; in the 1860s it took over 2 hours 30 minutes from Plymouth to Truro, officially getting in at 8.51 p.m., although it very often ran late.

Page 95. *Music and singing in the drawing room* There is a blank page left in the diary before this passage, and another before the beginning of the next day's entry, while all the following lines, including 'Children's voices', have been squeezed on to one page. The effect is thus curiously detached and self-contained – either because the contents held some particular significance for Kilvert, or else, more prosaically, because notes like this did not fit into the narrative and descriptive pattern of the diary as a whole, and he perhaps left the surrounding space for possible expansion of a thin entry for a day on which very little happened. Nevertheless, the passage offers fertile ground for speculation. All the songs that Kilvert records express sentimental romantic yearnings, but it is striking how many of them particularly involve themes of unfulfilled, and usually morally unattainable, love. One could take the entry as a deliberate, half-coded expression of Kilvert's intimate thoughts, like the Milton reference on 24 July; or as a piece of unconscious self-revelation; or as pure coincidence with no underlying significance. It would certainly be unwise to read too much into it (after all, such themes form the very staple of Victorian drawing-room songs), but the titles and verses that Kilvert has selected to record do suggest that, for him at least, his feelings for Emma Hockin imparted a sentimental *frisson* to the evening.

The first three songs (*Robin Adair, Ye Banks and Braes*, and *Annie Laurie*) have retained their popularity and need no comment.

Maggie's Secret ('Oh many a time I am sick at heart ...') was written and composed by 'Claribel' (Charlotte Aling-

ton Barnard, 1830–69), who produced about a hundred such pieces in the 1860s. The secret is that Maggie loves a sailor lad, and so rejects her village swains. In view of the fact that it was two summers since the Hockins had moved from Langley Burrell to Cornwall, it is curious to note that the second stanza begins:

Two summers ago when a brave ship sail'd
Far away to the golden west
O nobody knew that my heart went too
For the secret I never confess't ...

Susan's — In fact 'Susan's Story', also by Claribel ('Oh mother take the wheel away ...'). Susan loves a man who has just married another girl in preference to her. The ballad ends:

And afterwards we met and we were friendly all the same,
For ne'er a word I said to them of anger or of blame,
'Till both believ'd I did not care and, may be they were right —
But mother take the wheel away I cannot spin tonight.

The Carnival of Venice Presumably Julius Benedict's famous tune ('O me beata / Ritorna in ciel l'albore / Vo pormi un fiore in seno vo in cerca del mio amor ...'), of which there were several equally ludicrous English versions (e.g. 'O my beloved, / Far from me across the sea, / Come back and end my sadness, love of mine come back to me! ...'); unless Kilvert has given the wrong title to the following two lines, which are from Thomas Moore's 'Venetian Air' in his collection *National Airs* ('Oh, come to me when daylight sets; / Sweet! then come to me ...',

Poetical Works of Thomas Moore, edited by A.D. Godley [London, 1910], p.238).

Auld Robin Gray The well-known ballad: the girl narrator, believing her true love Jamie to be dead, has married Auld Robin Gray for security, when Jamie reappears, and she laments her plight. It is obviously very tempting to apply the lines that Kilvert quotes to his own situation (although no doubt not the whole story of the ballad). In fact he has interestingly misquoted the second line, part of a couplet which reads 'They gi'ed him my hand, but my heart was at the sea; / Sae auld Robin Gray is gude man to me' – i.e. husband, a deplorable state of affairs. Kilvert gives the girl the consolation of 'a good man', even though not the one she really loves. The first line quoted is from the end of the ballad: 'I dare nae think o' Jamie, for that would be a sin; / Sae I'll do my best a gude wife to be, / For Auld Robin Gray is kind to me.'

"No more she could weep ..." It has not proved possible to identify the source of these lines: they do not form part of the proper text of 'Auld Robin Gray'. It must be said that they could hardly be less appropriate to Emma Hockin, or indeed Kilvert, a salutary corrective perhaps to over-ingenious speculation about the other songs.

Page 95. *Children's voices* A theme that touched Kilvert. There are many similar references throughout the Diary, although they usually have more explanatory detail, e.g.: 'Went on up the dingle and the voices of the children of New Barn came merrily down the sheep meadow from where they were playing and laughing under the shadow of a hedge' (*NLW 1*, p.84).

Page 96. *Sorrowful dreams* An enigmatic and unexplained remark, particularly in this context. The text has evolved in several stages here. 'Redruth market' was writ-ten, by itself, at a different time from the previous paragraph and at a different angle on the page. Kilvert left a space beneath, then wrote the paragraph beginning 'We met with', probably at the same time. 'Sorrowful dreams' was written below 'Redruth market', again at a different time, with a different pen and much less firmly; while 'and people hurrying about with conger eels' has been squeezed in later still between the two. There are many similar examples of the successive elaboration of the text in this and the other two surviving notebooks, which make a fascinating study.

Page 96. *the British Church* St Gothian's (or Gwithian's) Chapel, probably first built in the sixth or seventh century, rebuilt and extended ninth – eleventh centuries, and abandoned in the thirteenth century because of the encroaching sand, when the present Parish Church was built. The ruins were completely buried by the middle of the eighteenth century, and accidentally exposed by a farmer digging a pond in 1827. They have now once more vanished beneath the shifting sands. The 'dissenting farmer' who discovered them was Richard Hockin of Churchtown Farm, a Methodist (at most a very distant relation to Kilvert's hosts – in the seventeenth century almost all the principal inhabitants of the area were called Cock or Hockin, and the name is very common). He roofed over the ruins and converted them into a cowshed. A considerable fuss was made in 1871 about the condition of the chapel, and moves undertaken to preserve it, although nothing subsequently came of them. The Revd Frederick Hockin was prominent in this, and Kilvert is no doubt to some extent reflecting the concern of his hosts. See Charles Thomas, *Gwithian* (Hayle, 1964), and Barry Smith, 'The Hockins and the British Church', *Kilvert Society Newsletter*, February 1989.

Page 98. *Mr Urquhart* The curate had only just arrived at Gwithian: the *West Briton* notes on Thursday 14 July 1870 that 'the Rev. Alexander Jolly Urquhart has been appointed assistant curate of Phillack and Gwithian' (p.4). His comments on his parishioners, although no doubt accurate enough, were thus very much a matter of first impressions.

Page 98. *the "severely correct" cruciform Church* This correctness was of very recent date. The original thirteenth-century church had been cruciform, but it had been much extended in the fifteenth century and a south aisle added. The sandstone and killas walls had deteriorated so much that the church had to be almost completely rebuilt in 1865–7, and the architect (Edmund Sedding of Penzance) restored the original shape while keeping the fifteenth-century tower. The reconstruction is generally sensitive and successful (the Revd Frederick Hockin met nearly the whole cost of the work himself), but this explains Kilvert's reference to fragments of the old church lying around. The lychgate is indeed remarkable, being assembled largely out of arches, principals, and assorted bits and pieces of the fifteenth-century south aisle.

Page 98. *a Mr Drury, who was drowned ...* Kilvert's account is accurate. What is truly surprising, though, is that for all his evident concern about the sad fate of a fellow-curate, Kilvert does not record the most startling detail of the whole tragedy: Drury had an eerie premonitory dream about his own death, which he related to one of the Hockins. It is very difficult to believe that, among so many other details, Kilvert was not also told this story by his hosts, and yet he makes no mention of it. He had left spaces in the notebook in this day's entry, as usual, and filled many in later; the note on Drury seems to be just filling such a gap, and perhaps there was simply no room to expand it further. It is worth quoting in full the report in the *West Briton* on Friday 14 April 1865, under the heading 'A Singular Dream, and a Clergyman Drowned':

> On Wednesday, the 5th inst., the Rev. Stephen Barclay Drury, an unmarried clergyman of 26, who had for about 12 months acted as the curate of Phillack and Gwithian, had a conversation with the brother of the rector of those parishes, Mr Charles Hockin, and related a dream, which he described as a very singular one, and as having made a deep impression on him. His words were:— "I dreamt I was to be buried, and I followed my coffin into the church, and thence to the tomb. I took no part in the service, and when we came to the tomb I looked into it and saw it was very nice. I then asked the undertaker who was to be buried, and he answered 'You'. I then said 'I am not to be buried – I am not dead'. The undertaker then said, 'I must be paid for the coffin'; upon which I awoke." On Sunday morning and afternoon Mr Drury officiated at Gwithian, and, after the second service, remained with the children to practice singing. Returning to his lodgings in Gwithian at half-past four, he waited a little, took with him Thomas a Kempis' "Christian Pattern", and set out for a walk, accompanied by a Newfoundland dog. He asked for a bit of cord, as he might give the dog a dip, and started in his usually cheerful and happy mood. In an hour and a half the dog returned, with the cord round his neck. Mr Drury was never again seen alive. His absence, throughout the night, occasioned no surprise, as he sometimes went to, and slept at Copperhouse, two miles off. On Monday morning, a Gwinear miner, in quest of seaweed at

low water, near the rocky shore of Godrevy saw a body in a pool 70 or 80 yards from the sea. Mr Drury's gold chain was about his neck and his watch-case: the workings of the watch had, apparently, been knocked out by the sea. His book was in his coat pocket; his hat was gone; and his pockets were filled with sand. The body was 40 yards from rocks about 30 feet high, and a pathway led from the precipitous cliffs above to these rocks. There was a cut over the right eye and in the head – such cuts as, in the opinion of experienced men, would be caused by a fall on rocks. Mr Drury was quite dead and stiff. An inquest, by the county coroner, Mr Roscorla, was held on Tuesday, at Gwithian, when these circumstances were elicited and a verdict was returned of "Found Drowned". From the facts however, that Mr Drury had never shown the least sign of depression – that he started with the expressed intention of giving the dog a dip – and that he was very near-sighted – the general inference is that the unfortunate gentleman slipped on the rocks, was stunned, fell into the water, and so casually and singularly fulfilled his strange dream of a few days previously.

(The reference to Charles Hockin is inaccurate: the Revd Frederick Hockin's brother Charles fell in action at Sidon in 1840. Drury must have told either one of his rector's other three surviving brothers; or his nephew Charles of the Truro branch; or possibly the Charles Hockin, son of Richard, who then owned Churchtown Farm.)

This dream of Drury's might give a darker colour to a humorous note in the Diary entry for 16 November 1870, which has always been seen as purely light-hearted: 'Last night the waning moon shone bright and cold in the East and I had a horrible dream that I was married to Mrs Danzey and living as curate at Gwythian. I woke up in a cold sweat' (I, 259) – the reference might be to Drury rather than to Urquhart.

The window to Drury's memory is the south window in the chancel.

Page 99. *a magnificent fruit-bearing fig tree* Only the huge stump remains. The tree had to be cut down around 1930, but it is well remembered by the very few elderly inhabitants who truly originate in the area. A seedling from the old tree is growing wild in a hedge in a lane south of the village, and there are apparently others to be found.

Page 100. *to look for sea anemones* cf. Emma Hardy on her childhood in Plymouth a decade earlier: 'there was a curious craze for sea-anemones then, everybody talking of, and collecting them' (*Some Recollections*, p.33).

Page 100. *"The last sigh of the moon"* This quotation has remained untraceable. The nearest approximation found to date is a stanza in Thomas Hood's 'Ode to Melancholy', in his *Poetical Works* (Oxford, 1935), p.191:

> The Moon! she is the source of sighs,
> The very face to make us sad;
> If but the world held nothing base,
> Of vile and mean, of fierce and bad;
> The same fair light that shone in streams,
> The fairy lamp that charm'd the lad;
> For so it is, with spent delights
> She taunts men's brains, and makes them mad.

The sentiments are not inappropriate, but the text is too distant to be convincing as the source of Kilvert's reference.

Page 100. *The last longing lingering farewell look*   The reference here is to Gray's Elegy:

> For who to dumb forgetfulness a prey,
> This pleasing anxious being e'er resigned,
> Left the warm precincts of the cheerful day,
> Nor cast one longing lingering look behind?

Page 101. *The "infant" Clare*   The Parkers' daughter, Clare Europa, was 14 years old, and born according to the Census returns in 'Gibraltar, Spain' (whence no doubt her unusual second name), where her father was serving as a Captain in 'Her Majesty's 3rd Regiment of Royal Lancashire Militia'. The quotation marks around the "infant" make it look like a family joke: perhaps a reference to the 'infanta'?

Page 101. *the tears of the morning*   Suggested by Coleridge's 'Youth and Age':

> Dew-drops are the gems of morning,
> But the tears of mournful eve!

Page 102. *the Holy Well*   This beautiful well is still as Kilvert described it, set against the hillside between the Falmouth Lodge and the Norway Inn, though now with more indirect access. It is generally called St Piran's Well, one of several in the area.

Page 103. *Cowper's "Tithing Time"*   A slight misquotation (as often) from the second stanza of 'The Yearly Distress; or, Tithing-time at Stock in Essex':

> This priest he merry is and blithe
>   Three quarters of the year,

> But oh! it cuts him like a scythe
>   When tithing time draws near.

Page 103. *The drooping of transplanted flowers*   Possibly suggested by some lines in Wordsworth's 'To A Distant Friend':

> Why art thou silent? Is thy love a plant
> Of such weak fibre that the treacherous air
> Of absence withers what was once so fair?

– but the idea is given a very different application here.

William Plomer notes that 'This last sentence is repeated almost exactly in the first entry of the next notebook, written on the same day at Langley Burrell', in *Kilvert's Cornish Holiday* (Hay-on-Wye: Kilvert Society, 1978), p.36. It looks as though Kilvert repeated it – at the beginning of the long nostalgic effusion that occupies the train journey back – as a deliberate link between the two notebooks. Plomer prints it in this latter context; the next notebook itself has of course been lost, like all the others after this Cornish Diary.

Bibliography

This is not a complete bibliography of Kilvert studies, nor of Cornwall in 1870. It lists the principal works which have provided information for this edition, and gives details of modern reprints of early works on Cornwall. Much interesting material relating to Kilvert and his Diary is to be found in the Kilvert Society's publications, including the *Kilvert Society Newsletter*: only the most directly relevant items are listed here. A further invaluable source of information has been contemporary newspapers, particularly *The Times*, the *West Briton and Royal Cornwall Gazette* (Truro), the *Falmouth Packet and Cornwall Advertiser* (Falmouth), and the *Cornish Telegraph* (Penzance).

Standard texts by English authors (Shakespeare, Milton, etc.) are not listed, but details of particular editions are given in the Notes where relevant. However, where an edition is referred to by Kilvert – such as Emma Hockin's copy of *The Idylls of the King* with Doré's illustrations – then it is listed below.

I. Manuscripts of Kilvert's Diary

Journal No. 2. 1870. From April 27th to June 10th. National Library of Wales, MS 21666A.
Journal No. 3. 1870. From June 11th to July 18th. National Library of Wales, MS 22090A.

Journal No. 4. 1870. From July 19th to August 6th. Cornwall. Durham University Library, Plomer Bequest.

II. Printed Works

(a) Kilvert's Diary

Kilvert's Diary: Selections from the Diary of the Rev. Francis Kilvert, chosen, edited and introduced by William Plomer, 3 vols (London: Cape, 1980; first published 1938–40).
The Diary of Francis Kilvert, April – June 1870, edited by Kathleen Hughes and Dafydd Ifans (Aberystwyth: National Library of Wales, 1982).
Kilvert's Cornish Holiday: Further Extracts from Kilvert's Diary, July 19th to August 6th 1870, transcribed by William Plomer (Hay-on-Wye: Kilvert Society, 1978).

(b) On Kilvert

Colloms, Brenda, *Victorian Country Parsons* (London: Constable, 1977).
Farmery, Eva, and R.B. Taylor, *Kilvert's 'Kathleen Mavourneen'* (Hay-on-Wye: Kilvert Society, 1980).
Fothergill, Robert A., *Private Chronicles: A Study of English Diaries* (London: Oxford University Press, 1974).

Grice, Frederick, *Francis Kilvert and His World* (Horsham: Caliban Books, 1982).

Grice, Frederick, 'Kilvert and Folklore', *Folklore*, 85 (Autumn 1974), pp.199–201.

Newman, C.W., 'Kilvert Unabridged: Review', *The Transactions of the Radnorshire Society*, 52 (1982), pp.80–90 (a review article on the edition of *NLW 1*).

O'Brien, Kate, *English Diaries and Journals* (London: Collins, 1943).

Plomer, William, 'Francis Kilvert and His Diary', in John Guest (ed.), *Essays by Divers Hands: being the Transactions of the Royal Society of Literature*, new series, 38 (London: Oxford University Press, 1975), pp.78–92.

Rowse, A.L., 'Kilvert in Cornwall', in *West Country Stories* (London: Macmillan, 1945), pp.145–60.

Rowse, A.L., 'Kilvert's Diary', in *The English Spirit* (London: Macmillan, 1946), pp.233–40.

Wyndowe, Mrs E.J. (Emily Kilvert), 'Rambling Recollections', in *More Chapters from the Kilvert Saga* (Hereford: Kilvert Society, n.d.), pp.84–126.

(c)   Other Works

Black's Guide to the Duchy of Cornwall (Edinburgh: A. & C. Black, 1876).

Blight, J.T., *Ancient Crosses and Other Antiquities in the West of Cornwall*, 3rd edn (London: Simpkin & Marshall, 1872).

Blight, J.T., *A Week at the Land's End*, 2nd edn (Penzance: 1876; reprinted Penzance: Alison Hodge, 1989. 1st edn 1861).

Blight, J.T., *Churches of West Cornwall* (Oxford: Parker, 1865).

Boase, G.C., *Collectanea Cornubiensia: A Collection of Biographical and Topographical Notes Relating to the County of Cornwall* (Truro: Netherton & Worth, 1890).

Borlase, William, *Antiquities Historical and Monumental of the County of Cornwall*, 2nd edn (London: 1769; reprinted with an introduction by P.A.S. Pool and Charles Thomas, Wakefield: EP Publishing, 1973. 1st edn 1754).

Bottrell, William ('An Old Celt'), *Traditions and Hearthside Stories of West Cornwall* (Penzance,· 1870; reprinted Newcastle upon Tyne: Frank Graham, 1970).

Canner, A.C., *The Parish of Tintagel: Some Historical Notes* (n.p., 1982).

Carter, Clive, *Cornish Shipwrecks: the North Coast* (Newton Abbot: David & Charles, 1970).

Chope, R. Pearse, *Early Tours in Devon and Cornwall*, reprinted with an introduction by Alan Gibson (Newton Abbot: David & Charles, 1967; first published 1918).

Collins, Wilkie, *Rambles Beyond Railways: Notes in Cornwall Taken A-Foot*, reprinted with an introduction by J.C. Trewin (London: Anthony Mott, 1982. A reprint of the London, 1861 edn; first published 1851).

Courtney, Miss M.A., *Cornish Feasts and Folk-Lore* (Penzance: Beare & Son, 1890).

Courtney, M.A., and T.Q. Couch, *Glossary of Words in Use in Cornwall*, English Dialect Society Series, no. 27 (London, 1880).

Cox, J. Charles, *County Churches: Cornwall* (London: George Allen, 1912).

Craik, Mrs, *An Unsentimental Journey through Cornwall* (London: Macmillan, 1884; reprinted Penzance: Patten Press, 1988).

Davy, Humphry, *The Poetry of Humphry Davy*, ed. Alison Pritchard (Penzance: Penwith D.C., 1978).

Douch, H.L., *The Book of Truro: A Portrait of the Town* (Chesham: Barracuda Books, 1977).

Dunstan, Bob, *The Book of Falmouth and Penryn* (Chesham: Barracuda Books, 1975).

Dunstan, Bob, *Falmouth's Famous Past* (Falmouth, 1968).

Falmouth Working Boats Association 1980 Souvenir Annual.

Gilbert, C.S., *An Historical Survey of the County of Cornwall*, 2 vols (Plymouth Dock, 1818–20).

Gilbert, Davies, *The Parochial History of Cornwall*, 4 vols (London: J.B. Nichols, 1838).

Grigson, Geoffrey, *The Englishman's Flora* (London: Phoenix House, 1955).

H., J.H., *Tourist's Guide to Penzance, Land's End, Logan Rock, St Michael's Mount, Kynance Cove, Lizard etc.* (Penzance: Rodda, 1875; first published 1873).

Hague, Douglas B., 'Early Lighthouses in Cornwall', *Cornish Archaeology*, no. 7 (1968), pp.64–7.

Hall, Nigel, 'Collecting Victorian Fern Books', *Antiquarian Book Monthly Review*, no. 109 (vol. 10, no. 5, May 1983), pp.170–5.

Hardy, Emma Lavinia, née Gifford, *Some Recollections: together with some relevant poems by Thomas Hardy*, eds Evelyn Hardy and Robert Gittings (London: Oxford University Press, 1961).

Harvey, E.G., *Mullyon: its History, Scenery, and Antiquities* (Truro: Lake, and London: Simpkin Marshall, 1875; reprinted Redruth: Dyllansow Truran, 1984).

Helps, Sir Arthur, *Friends in Council: a Series of Readings and Discourse Thereon*, 2 vols (London: Pickering, 1847).

Henderson, Charles, and Henry Coates, *Old Cornish Bridges and Streams* (Truro: Bradford Barton, 1972; first published 1928).

History Around the Fal, by the Fal History Group, 3 parts (University of Exeter, 1980–).

Hockin, J.C., 'The Hockin Family', *Kilvert Society Newsletter*, June 1984, pp.6–8.

Hooper, W. Tregoning, 'Perran Foundry and its Story', *The 106th Annual Report of the Royal Cornwall Polytechnic Society*, New Series, 9, part 3 (1939), pp.62–89.

Hudson, W.H., *The Land's End: a Naturalist's Impressions in West Cornwall*, 2nd edn (London: Hutchinson, 1911; reprinted London: Wildwood House, 1981).

Hunt, Robert, *Popular Romances of the West of England: or, the Drolls, Traditions, and Superstitions of Old Cornwall*, 3rd edn, revised and enlarged (London: Chatto & Windus, 1881; first published in two volumes in 1865).

James, Beryl, *John Knill: His Life and Times* (Redruth: Dyllansow Truran, 1980).

Jenkin, A.K. Hamilton, *Mines and Miners of Cornwall*, 14 parts (Truro: Truro Bookshop, 1961 *et seq.*).

Johns, Rev. C.A., *A Week at the Lizard*, 2nd edn (London: SPCK, 1873; first published 1848).

Karkeek, W.F., *The Report on the Farming of Cornwall, to which the Prize was awarded by the Royal Agricultural Society of England* (London: W. Clowes, 1846).

Lake, William, *A Complete Parochial History of the County of Cornwall*, 4 vols (Truro: Lake, and London: J.C. Hotten, 1867–72).

Larn, Richard, and Clive Carter, *Cornish Shipwrecks: the South Coast* (Newton Abbot: David & Charles, 1969).

MacDermot, E.T., *History of the Great Western Railway*, 2 vols (London: Great Western Railway Co., 1927–31).

Mackenzie, Compton, *My Life and Times, Octave 4, 1907–1915* (London: Chatto & Windus, 1965).

Morgan, W.E.T., *Radnorshire Words*, English Dialect Society Series, no. 32 (London, 1881).

Noall, Cyril, *The St Ives Mining District, I* (Redruth: Dyllansow Truran, 1982).

Noall, Cyril, and Graham Farr, *Wreck and Rescue Round the Cornish Coast*, 3 vols (Truro: Bradford Barton, 1964–6).

Padel, O.J., *Cornish Place-Name Elements* (Nottingham: English Place-name Society, 1985).

Padel, O.J., *A Popular Dictionary of Cornish Place-Names* (Penzance: Alison Hodge, 1988).

Pascoe, W.H., *C.C.C.: The History of the Cornish Copper Company* (Redruth: Dyllansow Truran, 1981).

Pevsner, Nikolaus, *The Buildings of England: Cornwall*, 2nd edn revised by Enid Radcliffe (Harmondsworth: Penguin Books, 1970: 1st edn 1951).

Polwhele, Richard, *The History of Cornwall*, 7 vols (London: Cadell & Davies, 1803–8; reprinted, with an introduction by A.L. Rowse, Dorking: Kohler & Coombes, 1978).

Pool. P.A.S., *The History of the Town and Borough of Penzance* (Penzance: The Corporation, 1974).

Procter, Ida, *Visitors to Cornwall* (Redruth: Dyllansow Truran, 1982).

Radford, C.A. Ralegh, *Tintagel Castle*, D.o.E. Official Handbook (London: HMSO, 18th impression, 1979: first published 1935).

Redding, Cyrus, *An Illustrated Itinerary of the County of Cornwall* (London: How & Parsons, 1842).

Romaunt, Christopher (i.e. J.F. Bowman), *The Island Home: or, the Young Cast-Aways* (London: Nelson, 1852).

Smith, Barry, 'The Hockins and the British Church', *Kilvert Society Newsletter*, February 1989, pp.7–11.

Smith, Barry, 'Rosewarne, the Parkers and the Lewises: Insanity, Imbecility and Inter-relationships in a Victorian Family', *Kilvert Society Newsletter*, September 1984, pp.7–12.

Smith, Barry, 'The Truro Hockins', *Kilvert Society Newslet-ter*, August 1985, pp.8–11.

Stevens, James, *A Cornish Farmer's Diary: Selections from the Diary of James Stevens of Zennor and Sancreed (1847–1918)*, ed. P.A.S. Pool (Penzance: the Editor, 1977).

Stockdale, F.W.L., *Excursions in the County of Cornwall* (London: Simpkin & Marshall, 1824).

Sullivan, B.J., 'Riviere House, Hayle', *Old Cornwall*, vol. 9 no. 3 (Autumn 1980), pp.118–27.

Tennyson, Alfred, *Idylls of the King*, illustrated by Gustave Doré (London: Moxon, 1868).

Thomas, Charles, *Gwithian* (Hayle: Mitchell, 1964).

Thomas, Charles, *Tintagel Castle* (London: English Heritage, 1986).

Thomas, Charles, ed., *Cornish Studies*, no. 16, Special Issue, 'Tintagel Papers' (Redruth: Institute of Cornish Studies, 1989).

Thomas, Charles, P.A.S. Pool, and Craig Weatherhill, *The Principal Antiquities of the Land's End District*, 16th edn (Penzance: Cornwall Archaeological Society, 1980; first published 1954).

Todd, A.C., and Peter Laws, *The Industrial Archaeology of Cornwall* (Newton Abbot: David & Charles, 1972).

Tregellas, Walter H., *Tourists' Guide to Cornwall and the Scilly Isles* (London: Edward Stanford, 1878).

Tregoning, E.S., *History of Falmouth* (Falmouth: Tregoning, 1865).

Warner, Rev. Richard, *A Tour through Cornwall in the Autumn of 1808* (Bath: R. Cruttwell, 1809).

Whetter, James, *The History of Falmouth* (Redruth: Dyllansow Truran, 1981).

Woodfin, R.J., *The Cornwall Railway to its Centenary in 1959* (Truro: Bradford Barton, 1972; first published 1960).

Sources of Illustrations

The editors and publishers would like to thank all those who gave so generously of their time, and knowledge of nineteenth-century Cornwall, and who allowed us to reproduce illustrations.

The sources of illustrations are as follows: the British Library, *no. 67*; Cornwall County Library, Cornish Studies Library, Redruth, *nos. 23, 25, 41–3, 48, 50, 58, 63 and 73*; the Francis Frith Collection (from a postcard in the collection of Eric Richards), *no. 45*; John Hockin, *nos. 2–5*. James Hodge, *nos. 10, 27, 37–9, 46–7, 49, 52, 55–6, 61, 65, 71 and 72*; the Kilvert Society, *no. 1*; the National Trust, *no. 64*; the Osborne Collection, Royal Cornwall Polytechnic Society, Falmouth, *no. 21*; Penzance Town Council, Penlee House Museum and Art Gallery, Penzance, *nos 34, 44 and 68*; the Royal Institution of Cornwall, *nos. 11–20, 22, 24, 28–33, 36, 40, 51, 53, 57, 59, 60, 66, 69 and 70*; Michael Trinick, *nos. 26, 35 and 62*; the University of Durham Library, *nos. 6–9. No. 54* Copyright reserved. Reproduced by gracious permission of Her Majesty The Queen. Turner's painting of St Michael's Mount, on the *front cover*, is reproduced by courtesy of the Board of Trustees of the Victoria & Albert Museum.

Index